"I've been deeply involved with New York City for more than sixty years, but reading Owen Hatherley's book — the result of a mere two visits — makes me feel as if I'd just gotten off the bus from Rubeville. I'd known about what were generally called the projects, but hadn't realized there were so many, of such variety, built by so many different entities. Hatherley lays out the great social-democratic city-state that briefly flourished in the 1950s and 60s, only to be thoroughly ravaged by private interests in the following decades. It filled me with retroactive pride."

LUCY SANTE, AUTHOR OF *LOW LIFE* AND
I HEARD HER CALL MY NAME

"What a prospect: Owen Hatherley goes West — into the Great Satan. He's armed with sarcasm, socialism, sturdy shoes. And the spectral company of Marshall Berman, Samuel Delany, the GZA, Michael Sorkin. He takes on the New York Ideology and its sacred cows. He celebrates a little-known fact: New York has more cheap public housing than anywhere else in North America. As always, he's a skewer and a seer."

SUKHDEV SANDHU, AUTHOR OF *NIGHT HAUNTS*
AND *LONDON CALLING*

T0282275

WALKING THE STREETS/WALKING THE PROJECTS

WALKING THE STREETS/WALKING THE PROJECTS

Adventures in Social Democracy in NYC and DC

Owen Hatherley

Published by Repeater Books

An imprint of Watkins Media Ltd

Unit 11 Shepperton House

89-93 Shepperton Road

London

N1 3DF

United Kingdom

www.repeaterbooks.com

A Repeater Books paperback original 2024

1

Distributed in the United States by Random House, Inc., New York.

ISBN: 9781915672445

Ebook ISBN: 9781915672452

Printed and bound by CPI Group (UK) Ltd, Croydon, CR0 4YY, United Kingdom.

CONTENTS

"New York is evil at its core."[1]

Cannibal Ox

"I have no family tree. The only member of my family who has is my dog Yank. He is the son of Doughboy, who was the son of Siegfried, who was the son of Tannhäuser, who was the son of Wotan. A distinguished family tree, to be sure — but after all, he's only a son of a bitch."[2]

Fiorello La Guardia

"I don't drink coffee, I take tea my dear."[3]

Quentin Crisp, via Sting

Introduction
The New York Ideology

New York, like Paris, is paradise for a particular kind of urbanist. Unlike the French capital, it is not exactly a paragon of architectural preservation or coherence, but it has similarly attracted writers who like walking, and who like to pile a particular kind of theory upon walking. People do not write about Manchester or Detroit or San Diego or Madrid or Tokyo or Buenos Aires or Athens or Delhi or Chengdu or Melbourne or even London in the way that they write about New York and Paris. This is partly owed to their prominence in the culture industry, and in the mythologies of modern art — if for Walter Benjamin Paris was *Capital of the Nineteenth Century*, New York was *Capital of the Twentieth Century*, at least according to Kenneth Goldsmith in his imitative book of fragments. New York, we are told, "stole" modern art from Paris sometime after the Second World War, with the aid of the Central Intelligence Agency. New York and Paris are written about as cities that are unique, but also quintessential — special, not like the city you live in, but also the Urban Experience condensed and purified. Lessons from them are applied to everywhere else.

The Parisian version of this is a congeries of Walter Benjamin, André Breton, Guy Debord, *Nouvelle Vague* films and *Emily in Paris*, and need not detain us further. The New York approach is summed up most of all in the writing of the Scranton, Pennsylvania-raised *savant* Jane

Jacobs, and her disciples, who are found both on the political left — Marshall Berman, Michael Sorkin — and on the political right, such as Edward Glaeser and a legion of extremely online "YIMBYs" and "market urbanists". It is a small and not entirely representative group, but it tends to monopolise discussion of the city, and particularly how it is interpreted abroad. Not all writers about New York's architecture and urbanism are exponents of this New York Ideology — Lewis Mumford, for instance, might have lived in New York all his life and written about it voluminously, but with his love of garden city planning, his undying hatred of *laissez faire* and the slums, and his passionate belief that it is better to be bored than to be poor, he is the ideology's anthesis. The New York Ideology centres on a titanic battle that apparently took place in the 1960s between two figures — the urban tsar Robert Moses, and the campaigner Jane Jacobs.[1] This story has been endlessly told and retold in everything from documentary films to comic books. New York is the only city which could produce a book such as *The Power Broker*, a thousand pages on one urban bureaucrat, and regard it as the last word on city planning.[2]

The New York Ideology — we could call it the Street Ideology, so much does it obsess about pavements — is an exciting way of reading and understanding the city. It privileges, and politicises, direct observation. The primal scene of the New York Ideology is the ordinary, middle-class Greenwich Village resident Jane Jacobs realising that city planning as it was then understood was based on a lie, because it looked like a lie. She walked from the "slum" of the Village, with its conviviality, noise and activity — much of which faced potential annihilation by Moses' Lower Manhattan Expressway — to the places she called "the projects". She was not impressed. Over time, the term "projects" came to describe only public housing estates in

American vernacular, but Jacobs' use was more expansive: projects were those places which had been planned as one large ensemble by a public or private authority. These ranged from council estates in Harlem to luxury flats in Midtown Manhattan to cultural centres in the Upper West Side. They were all, Jacobs argued, based on a misunderstanding of how cities worked. Most people understood cities organically, in an unplanned, grassroots way, and when they came across these single-use, monolithic zones they simply voted with their feet and either stayed in their homes or walked somewhere else. This argument came to be expanded into the claim that such places spelled doom for urban economies, which would collapse under the weight of big bureaucracy or big business.

That mission creep into positions which seem to be patently obviously neoliberal is why I have always found Jacobs frustrating to the point of being sometimes unreadable, but in around half of her *The Death and Life of Great American Cities*, and especially the essays that preceded it, like the brilliant "Downtown Is for People", the appeal is obvious:

> the underlying intricacy, and the life that makes downtown worth fixing at all, can never be fostered synthetically. No one can find what will work for our cities by looking at the boulevards of Paris, as the City Beautiful people did; and they can't find it by looking at suburban garden cities, manipulating scale models, or inventing dream cities. You've got to get out and walk. Walk, and you will see that many of the assumptions on which the projects depend are visibly wrong.[3]

Yes, you can understand the city from using your eyes and your ears, no you don't need any special knowledge and least of all a sinecured position to do so.

A Street — Hell's Kitchen, Manhattan

This is taken to a more generalised level still in Marshall Berman's great 1982 book *All That Is Solid Melts Into Air*, which centres on two projects of the mythic Robert Moses — the creation of Jones Beach in Long Island out of a poisoned wasteland in the 1940s, and the destruction of the South Bronx by the "meat axe" of the Cross-Bronx Expressway forced through the borough in the 1960s. Berman's book takes in Marx, Baudelaire and much else in an elliptical history of "the experience of modernity", favouring a "Modernism in the streets" over some putative high Modernism of planners and fancy art galleries — but it is all rooted in growing up in New York City and walking, walking, walking. Just a few years earlier, Rem Koolhaas, an out-of-towner from all the way in Rotterdam, published *Delirious New York*, a "retroactive manifesto" for a capitalist city too moronic to ever really understand its own outlandish and astounding achievements: a hymn to the multifunctional skyscraper complexes created by the Manhattan grid and the New York Zoning Code, with a series of conformist WASP architects as the unknowing vessels for the architectural Id.

There are aspects of the New York Ideology that are about more than a particular way of walking and understanding the city. Another comes from the peculiar artistic explosion that happened there during the 1970s, particularly in the Downtown art and music scene. The first wave of punk, where people who looked like they subsided on gruel and cigarettes gamely tried to fuse Arthur Rimbaud, the Brill Building and Sonny Sharrock in three-minute bursts; its transformation into the nihilistic barrage of No Wave, an attempt to end pop music altogether in a burst of untrained noise and rage; the panoramic, edge-of-chaos sweep of Talking Heads' *Remain in Light*; the Cole Porter goes to Studio 54 world of Mutant Disco. And if this was all happening Downtown, then in the South Bronx, the place described with such love and rage by Marshall Berman, hip-hop was being invented by young, black, working-class people, rather than the newly-arrived Connecticut hipsters who were behind punk and No Wave. All of this music displayed an incredible appetite for Modernist invention, but its view of the city differed according to class and race. It could be a place to escape to from the rest of the USA ("I'm gonna get on that train and go to New York City and I'm gonna be somebody", rapped a punk poet raised in New Jersey), and it could be a place to which you were condemned ("I got no money to move out, I guess I got no choice", rapped a pioneering MC from the South Bronx).[4] If you can trace a line from one of these movements to the gentrification-rock of the Strokes, the other leads you by the 1990s to works of depth and power like *Illmatic*, *Liquid Swords*, *Only Built 4 Cuban Linx...* and *The Cold Vein*, each a little Modernist novel about creatively interpreted misery in the metropolis.

Almost all of this culture comes from the 1970s and early 1980s, which was the decade in which the richest and most powerful city in the world faced a shocking financial collapse — narrowly avoiding bankruptcy — soon followed by blackouts, riots, looting and the incineration of much of the Bronx by rogue landlords. It is often summed up by a photo in which the hapless mayor of New York City, Abraham Beame, held up a newspaper with the headline, "FORD TO CITY — DROP DEAD", on the day President Gerald Ford refused to bail out the greatest American metropolis. It's this cityscape you can see, redolent of a combination of Fritz Lang's *Metropolis* and an Eastern European city recently subjected to aerial bombing, in the background of films like *Wild Style*, *The Warriors* and *Escape from New York*.

I hope it will be obvious in the following essay that I love all this culture. I grew up on it; I would take the low Modernism of *Remain in Light* or *Liquid Swords* in a heartbeat over the entire output of most high Modernist composers, painters, architects and planners. What it all adds up to is something that is, first, incredibly democratising and liberating — that you can understand the world, and the economy, and politics, through walking the city, and making art and music about that experience. Anyone can do it — the city is yours. But after that, it is debilitating and limiting, because of the political and economic story it tells. The great unplanned, unconscious, untrammelled city made a terrible mistake, it tells you — it tried to plan itself and change itself, in the form of those expensive "projects". New York was almost brought down by such hubris, and the city was saved from the 1980s onwards by, on street level, the incredible grassroots pop culture that emerged out of the crisis, and from above, by the demented return of *Delirious New York*, in the form of a real estate and finance boom given concrete form by the likes of the developer, oompa-loompa-like Surrealist art object and future far-right President Donald Trump, a man whose mannerisms and accent, not to mention his cruel and bizarre sense of humour, are far more New York than any other American president.

The New York Ideology is inclusive. Its exponents, Jane Jacobsians all, range from the black queer science fiction writer Samuel R. Delany on its far-left, to James Howard Kunstler, the grumpily conservative theorist of a small-town New Urbanism, on its far-right. But in either case, social change does not, or should not, occur through the actions of a consciously planning, active state. The only way the New York Ideology envisages housing becoming affordable is through some sort of economic or natural disaster emptying the buildings so that you can squat them. The fact that New York has more permanently affordable public and social housing than anywhere else in North America is of interest only in the origin stories of MCs ("my whole crew is lounging/celebrating every day/no more public housing"[5]). The city is for you, says the New York Ideology; just don't think about changing it.

When something culturally important happens on a *street*, it does so because it has been enabled by the street, and its unique propensity to channel, intensify and diversify urban life. When something culturally important happens in a *project*, like, say, the creation of the USA's most successful popular music of the last forty years, it has happened in spite of the project and of the deadening hand of high Modernist planning. Both sides of New York's current planning debates are New York Ideologists: "NIMBYs" for whom the local community's voice is final and always knows what is best for it; so too "YIMBYs", with their touching belief that the untamed free market, if it were only unleashed even more than it already is, would make housing affordable.

What is irritating about the New York Ideology, and its Parisian cousin, is that it swamps any understanding of cities that are not New York (or Paris), as the incredibly seductive and exciting way of reading urban space developed in each is applied to places which aren't much like either of these two rather unusual cities. British intellectuals in the London Boroughs of Camden and Islington in the 1970s talked about Jane Jacobs and "the stoop"[6] in a damp, introverted city where buildings do not have "stoops" and public life is more likely to take place in the pub or the park than on the street. Londoners lament "radiant garden city beautiful" while enjoying a walk through a metropolis which almost disappears into the trees when seen from a high level. Stockholmers living in socialised housing better than anything ever built by a free market pontificate about the terrible effects of big state planning. Berliners denounce the malevolent Moses-like man in the town hall when, as recently as the early 1990s, their own men and women in the town hall handed anarchists the keys to dozens of disused buildings. These cities, which were shaped to a remarkable degree by social democracy in the twentieth century, simply can't be understood through the filter of Manhattan. The New York Ideology is very little use in understanding places that are not New York. But what I wanted to know is this: how useful is it in understanding New York itself?

Walk 1
Paleotechnical Manhattan

It is astonishing how popular New York remains as a place to visit, given how much misery it immediately inflicts upon you when you arrive. As I found on arrival in late 2014, JFK Airport is an enormous unfunny joke about the wonders of market competition — a complex of badly connected termini run by different airlines, with a monorail running between them but no direct public transport connection to the city. If, in New York's golden age as *Capital of the Twentieth Century*, its arrivals approached by sea, watching the skyscrapers gradually coming into focus above the waters — an effect of awe probably comparable in human history only to that of the pyramids — now you can see that skyline only in the far distance as you land. Next, you are forced to shuffle through a series of grey sheds, moving at a crawling pace through long, long queues in narrow, low-ceilinged corridors. I have never been looked at with such suspicion by such a hard-faced border control as I have upon entering the United States, and I've been a dozen times to Russia. One salutary effect is giving a little sense of what crossing borders is like for most of the world's population — you constantly feel in JFK that one false move will make the Men in Black disappear you. After the AirTrain "transit" (noun) that tootles around the airport and its exurban environs finally deposits you in the Subway station which will take you from Queens to Manhattan, you can take

The Lights at the End of the Tunnel

a look around the state of the USA's largest city's public transport.

Sutphin Boulevard station was opened in 1982. The design was by Hellmuth, Obata and Kassabaum, a corporate Brutalist firm from St Louis that gradually diversified into the construction of sports megastadiums. The station, with its exposed concrete and tile, was designed much earlier, with the initial plans dating from 1968; this is a 1960s building realised after a decade of fiscal austerity, and looks it. It is narrow, with a curious concrete ceiling which overhangs toward the platforms. The hall tapers as you walk along, until at the furthest point it is as tight as one of the Glasgow Subway's Hobbiton stations. It is exceptionally dark — although not so dark that you can't see how damp and stained everything is — and lit by some hilarious little upturned lampshades which you can imagine hanging melancholically from the ceiling of a bedsit. Welcome to America, ladies and gents.

The queue at Ellis Island wouldn't have been nice either. There was plenty of filth to be seen when the migrants were deposited in the slums of Lower Manhattan. But in the twenty-first century, JFK is an airport that would embarrass Kyrgyzstan or Moldova. It is unsurprising that the tycoon and reality TV star threatening to stand for President would soon be making a redress of the humiliating state of American airports part of his case for "Making America Great Again". When Trump compared the country's airports — particularly those of New York — to those of "a third world country", the *Economist*, the magazine of the class that flies a great deal, described this, understandably, as "an understatement".[1] The immediate impression of the USA here is a predictable one — a country where public space is treated as badly as it could possibly be while continuing to (just about) function, and where any large-scale planning is carried out with the utmost ineptitude. I make my way through the Subway, eventually get out at night from a station in the Upper West Side of Manhattan, check in, and go to sleep.

And then you wake up. I first visited in late November, as autumn turned to winter — blue skies, hard, cold air, the buildings crisply outlined. If it appears as you trudge through the city's public transport that you are in an impoverished city, a walk in the Upper West Side will divest you of this misapprehension with great speed. The pavements are wide, elegantly paved. Buildings are opulent, clean, in excellent condition; the few cars are large and expensive; even the entrances to the Subway, with their big Helvetica signs and colour-coded letters and numbers for the separate lines, look excellent. No wonder these people are so obsessed with the street, given the contrast between above and below. The first buildings I see are a clutch of enormous early-twentieth-century luxury apartment blocks, Classical in their details but nonetheless rectangular, sheer-sided, grid-like, looking like they're just waiting for Modernism to be invented, with a few more elaborate, florid edifices. One of these immediately stopped me in my tracks — the Ansonia, designed by the French architect Paul Emile Duboy, and built between 1899 and 1903.

It is modern — a high-rise building with a steel frame, serviced by lifts — but it looks antiquated, like a block of Oxford Circus or Regent Street has been reconstituted, with each building piled on top of the other until it reaches seventeen storeys, or a Parisian hotel stretched upwards by a child using Photoshop. There is no attempt to make it into a single tower with an upwards momentum, as American designers like Louis Sullivan were attempting in Chicago at the same time. Instead, European Good Taste is stretched out on such a vast, non-European scale that its motifs and proportions become incomprehensible and bizarre, with the cupolas the same size as a building one-quarter of its height. Until it was turned into a luxury apartment block in the Nineties, the Ansonia was a hotel,[2] and gradually fell into interesting desuetude in that all-important period of brilliant and appalling "decline" in the Sixties and Seventies. It became famous for a gay bath house, the Continental Baths, where revellers were entertained by a young Bette Midler and Barry Manilow, and for a gay club, Plato's Retreat. The shopping arcade was known for a concentration of pornographers and fortune-tellers. Its owners spent a while trying to get it demolished, but pressure from preservationists saw them redevelop the Ansonia as flats; now, it's just another place among many around here where very rich people live, which is just what it was always meant to be. A sign in front, dangling from the lamppost, reads, "NYC: SHOP SMALL IN THE BIG CITY". Municipal Jane Jacobs propaganda!

Baby's First Building Cake

From here, I walk down Broadway to my first "project" — Lincoln Center. This is the original Modernist cultural centre, preceding by a couple of years the likes of London's Southbank Centre or Berlin's Kulturforum; a consciously

planned miniature district full of concert halls. As
architecture, it is immediately noticeable as vastly more
conservative than either of these. The first sight shows
a Modernism diluted to the point of Neoclassicism, with
colonnaded marble blocks framing a square, in the manner
of a slightly updated EUR in Rome. The buildings date from
1962 and were completed in 1966; the main monuments,
those columned, gleaming edifices, are the round-arched
Metropolitan Opera House, designed by Wallace K.
Harrison, the Avery Fisher Hall (now the David Geffen
Hall) by Max Abramovitz, and the New York State Theater
(now the David H. Koch Theater) by Philip Johnson.
Deeper exploration will bring you to Eero Saarinen's more
straightforwardly Modernist Vivian Beaumont Theater,
but that is no more exciting.

By now all this has a certain *period charm*, especially since
Mad Men made the most joyless corporate "mid-century
Modernism" into the new Art Deco for upwardly mobile
collectors. The marble and the Classical proportions are joined
with large expanses of glass and spacious, flowing foyers,
though they are staid and stuffy compared with, say, London's
Royal Festival Hall, designed over a decade earlier; however,
closer inspection will reveal that its art patronage was a little
more adventurous for its time than its architecture, with
a Henry Moore and a pool framing the Vivian Beaumont
Theater. The coherence of the ensemble is impressive, and the
use of great sheets of marble, while pretentious and obvious,
also creates a certain icy, abstract grandeur, especially in
the cold, clear November weather. But here, you might find
yourself asking whether the New York Ideology, in spurning
this place as a failure (despite the enormous quantity of
people who have used, and continue to use, these buildings),
has a little bit of a point. There's little metropolitan energy and
crackle here — everything has been frozen into place, a series
of hard monuments around an empty space.

Arcades. Project

Tickertape Public Realm

Jane Jacobs designated Lincoln Center as a typical "project", despite the fact it did not directly entail any housing (though there is much near the site, with luxury blocks directly overlooking the theatres, and public housing behind it), because it aimed to do one thing, just one thing. Rather than building some theatres on Broadway, it is a Cultural District, a complete, zoned entity, where culture exists in a special reservation rather than as part of the city's everyday life. As she wrote in "Downtown Is for People", "this cultural superblock is intended to be very grand and the focus of the whole music and dance world of New York", but is not plugged into the streets, and shows little understanding of either how public space actually works or how people might use it; no restaurants, no florists, no pubs. Lincoln Center's "eastern street is a major trucking artery where the cargo trailers, on their way to the industrial districts and tunnels, roar so loudly that sidewalk conversation must be shouted".[3] Well, the industrial districts are not industrial anymore, so that problem has been removed. What Jacobs does not mention in this particular essay (though she alludes to it elsewhere) is the process by which this gleaming enclave was created. What is now Lincoln Center was in the 1950s a mainly black and Puerto Rican neighbourhood, which was slum-cleared over the course of that decade under the direction of Robert Moses, with residents moved to public housing towers elsewhere in Manhattan. Allegedly, the demolition of the tenements that previously occupied the site was delayed so they could form an appropriately grimy desolate backdrop to *West Side Story*.

It is hard, in most European cities of the time, to imagine that an electorate would tolerate the erasure of an entire working-class district for the sake of some opera houses. What is also highly unusual in the formation of Lincoln Center is the crucial role of one family, the Rockefellers.

Once you've looked up how a particular twentieth-century New York landmark has come into being, you will usually find that the Rockefellers and their money are lurking in the background or the foreground somewhere, to the point where, after a while, the focus on Jacobs and Moses seems like a smokescreen to divert you from this glaring fact; as Robert Fitch argued in his 1996 *The Assassination of New York*, describing this city in the twentieth century without the Rockefellers is like telling the story of Singapore without Lee Kuan Yew.

At the end of the nineteenth century, the Philadelphia-based German-American John D. Rockefeller founded Standard Oil, an enormous multinational petroleum firm which after many breakups and mergers became ExxonMobil, one of those American Big Oil giants that are currently busy trying to ensure that much of the planet becomes uninhabitable over the next few decades. Son John D. Jr got into property development and philanthropy, while grandsons John D. III, Nelson and David became major philanthropists, politicians and bankers, respectively, with Nelson Rockefeller serving several terms as (Republican) governor of New York State before becoming Gerald Ford's vice-president. Their fingerprints are almost everywhere. Lincoln Center was John D. Rockefeller III's baby, and he chaired the foundation that created it for the first decade of its existence. The usual credit for the complex that is granted to Moses is undeserved; as Fitch pointed out, "so little leverage did Moses have, he wasn't even invited to the dedication ceremonies, which were presided over by John D. Rockefeller III".[4]

Perhaps to expiate some of these many sins, Lincoln Center has, you'll find on exploring the buildings, been subject to a comprehensive programme of fashionable civic enlivening over the last couple of decades. A sign in the window of one of the buildings tells you this, with the words "PUBLIC SPACE" outlined in front of a schematic drawing of a tree. The improvements to the Center were designed by the then extremely fashionable firm of Diller, Scofidio and Renfro between 2003 and 2010, and they litter the complex in a seemingly deliberately incoherent, surrealist, ultra-mediated way. On the plaza, LED strips of lettering inset into the steps read out what you can find inside the buildings — "Family Events/Fashion/Theater/ Vocal Music". A fan-shaped, partially grassed impromptu amphitheatre occupies another corner. Most fun of all is the redesigned skyway that reaches over the street from the plaza to one of the Center's more abstract, introverted peripheral buildings, the Juilliard School of Music, adding some of the multi-level excitement you might find in the Southbank Centre. Walking across it is a relief after all this heavy Neoclassicism, and offers a flattering view of the

Instant Amphitheatre

complex's coherence among the messier tangle of streets and housing towers around.

The LED signs on the steps are maybe a little nod to the sort of supergraphics for which a certain area nearby is known. Times Square is a cornerstone of the New York Ideology — its finest exponent, Marshall Berman, devoted his last book, *On the Town*, to this intersection, a cluster of theatres and cinemas (and, for a time, sex shops and porn cinemas and cruising spaces) which has been immortalised in a century of films and musicals and showtunes. In urban history — leaving aside for a moment its gay history, recorded in Samuel R. Delany's *Times Square Red, Times Square Blue* — it is significant as the heartland of neon, one of the first places to be treated as a gigantic three-dimensional advertisement landscape. Berman, remembering how his mother would travel on the Subway from the Bronx to Times Square in order to "take a bath of light", goes into understandable contortions to reconcile his love for the kinetic glamour of this zone with his commitment to socialism and anti-capitalism. Rhapsodising about the LED Nasdaq sign that once hung here, he claimed that "its adventurous graphics were loved and mourned mainly by people who had little love for its market values"[5] (he might, and I might agree, but otherwise how could he possibly know?). He defends the "cleaning up" and rebuilding of the area by a consortium of developers, and in a particularly sad moment, the elderly, diminutive, bearded and very casually dressed Berman recalls being bundled out of a new Times Square department store under the presumption of being a tramp.[6]

Each of the two major writers on Times Square has their own utopia, their own moment when the square was at its best — the 1940s and 1950s for Berman, when this was a neon-lit theatreland for all the working-class family, and for Delany, the 1970s and 1980s, when it was a place

Times Square Red, Times Square Blue

where middle-aged working-class men could happily sit in a cinema and wank each other off all afternoon. Dialectics aside, Berman essentially approved the taming of the place from its Seventies sleaze peak/nadir, and its transformation during the 1990s back into the more corporate, big-business space it originally was. Unlike Delany, Berman found nothing utopian in the sex industry district this had become by the Eighties. But Delany's is the better book. *Times Square Red, Times Square Blue* is every bit as rooted in *The Death of Life of Great American Cities* as *On the Town*, and wholly shares the New York Ideology's spatial determinism, its cartoonish account of twentieth-century city-planning and its undeservedly forgiving attitude towards landlords, but does something much more interesting with Jacobs' ideas than most.

Times Square Red, Times Square Blue is easily ridiculed — "how Jane Jacobs explains why you should be able to go to a cinema to masturbate with strangers" — but it is rooted in an extremely in-depth analysis of a real place and real interactions. For Delany, the sleazy Times Square was actually an exemplar of what Jacobs calls "contact" — as opposed to "networking" — the cross-class meetings and encounters that you can only find in a metropolis, and which differentiate it from a small town or a village. Of the porn cinemas of Seventies/Eighties Times Square, Delany writes,

> Since I started frequenting them in the summer of 1975, I've met playwrights, carpenters, opera singers, telephone repair men, stockbrokers, guys on welfare, guys with trust funds, guys on crutches, on walkers, in wheelchairs, teachers, warehouse workers, male nurses, fancy chefs, guys who worked at Dunkin Donuts, guys who gave out flyers on street corners, guys who drove garbage trucks, and guys who washed windows on the Empire State Building. As a gentile, I note that this is the only place in a lifetime's New York residency I've had any extended conversation with some of the city's Hasidim.[7]

He feared that the redevelopment of this extremely complex space (with its "groceries, drugstores, liquor stores, dry cleaners, diners, and specialty shops ranging from electronics stores and tourist shops to theatrical memorabilia and comic book stores, interlarding a series of theaters, film and stage, rehearsal spaces, retailers of theatrical equipment, from lights to makeup, inexpensive hotels, furnished rooms, and restaurants at every level, as well as bars and the sexually oriented businesses") would become "a ring of upper-middle-class luxury apartments around a ring of tourist hotels clustering about a series of theaters and restaurants" centring on a "large mall and a cluster of office towers".[8] The reason for this disaster was a small-town ideology which asserted that the most important thing a city could be — aside from profitable — was "safe", belying the obvious fact that, as anybody who has watched the news in the last twenty years must be aware, America's small towns are far more violent than the Moloch of Manhattan. He has concrete proposals, too, advocating that the area be gradually reconstructed with a series of public spaces specifically for sex, which rather closely resemble the "Love Hotels" that are common in Tokyo or Osaka. Berman, however, found himself literally advocating his own social cleansing — one of the sadder outcomes of the left's adherence to its own version of the New York Ideology.

Well, Times Square now is full of big chain stores and hotels, and they're every bit as dull as Delany had warned. Some of the hotels are more *architecturally* interesting than others. My eye naturally went immediately to John Portman's Marriott Marquis, New York's only example of this architect-developer's wilfully dystopian, Piranesian, introverted, late-modern architecture. It was commenced in the early 1970s, lay derelict and unfinished for many years during the New York Fiscal Crisis, and opened in the

24

new Reaganite dawn of the 1980s, to which it seems well-suited. To the street, it is a fortress, two skyscraping wings of sheer concrete, the hotel rooms in stepped glass blocks within a vast grey sandwich. Inside is one of Portman's

The Hotel Dystopia

great dystopian interiors, with its glass pod lifts rocketing up and down a sinister atrium. Other hotels nearby are much blander, this sort of dramatising of the conjuncture being a little surplus to requirements.

Aside from the simple effects of congestion — the way thousands of people are channelled into it by Broadway's angle in the grid — Times Square is unexciting, after all you have been told about it. The straightforward objection is that you're just looking at digital kipple, invasive smartphone ads bursting into your actual space. The jaded traveller's objection to it, meanwhile, is that if you've been to any big city in East Asia this is vanilla stuff, neon and ads still relatively respecting the architecture and the buildings' scale: nothing so gloriously seedy as the grimy lightboxes and anime characters of an Akihabara or a Shinjuku, nothing so pulsating and rippling as the night-time lightshow of Shanghai or Seoul. In Tokyo, this place would have several anime department stores, some record shops, cafés full of people in weird outfits, a selection of odd restaurants in basements or at the top of skyscrapers, a load of sex shops and a dozen Love Hotels to warm Delany's heart. The torch of this sort of unpredictable cyber-modernity has long since been passed to Asia, and on that level, Times Square now looks like a mere Piccadilly Circus. This is obviously a result of the Disneyfication (literally — the Walt Disney Corporation were one of the major investors in the remodelled square) that has taken place here. It is now the world of M&M's World and Hershey's World. In some ways, Portman's building started the rot — the authors of the *AIA Guide to the Architecture of New York City* note that it entailed the demolition of three Broadway theatres. "Perhaps this is their tombstone."[9]

Many of the famous modern buildings of Midtown Manhattan are similarly a little underwhelming, if for very different reasons. For instance: Mies van der Rohe's

Seagram Building, the great Modernist skyscraper, the epitome of minimalist elegance, takes a fair bit of finding among a rack of copycat Miesian towers. And yes, its proportions and its detailing are better than these, but any effect of contrast in its visual restraint and its setting back from the streetline behind a framing plaza has been long since lost.[10] The Fifties kitsch typeface of the "BRASSERIE" roots it as much in its time as Lincoln Center. It is the pre-1945 buildings that still feel alien and thrilling round here. Weaving in and out of Broadway and into and out of Central Park, it is the antiquated, sentimental, dreamlike and bizarre that kept dragging my eye upwards. It is also here that you will find the most unique architecture, at least in the sense of buildings that have no analogue in the Old World. Much of this is drearily familiar to the average New Yorker but exotic to anyone else, from the cast-iron escape staircases upwards. Most of all, those cylindrical, spindly-legged, sometimes conical water tanks on top of every building are monuments in themselves, little Bernd and Hilla Becher industrial miniatures on top of brick tenements and stone-clad skyscrapers alike.

As your eye scans the rooflines, they become part of a fascinating steampunk junkshop. I could identify the twin neo-Spanish Empire cupolas on top of the luxury apartments of Emery Roth's 1930 San Remo Towers, overlooking Central Park, the magnificent Verdigris skyway of Gimbel's Bridge, a three-storey passageway of 1925 suspended ten storeys in the air, and the shining green copper saltshakers on top of the Waldorf Astoria. But going through Paul Goldberger and the AIA's guides to Manhattan architecture couldn't help me identify the ridiculous rose window in the sky surrounded with bare grey brick on one skyscraper roof, or the trees growing out of the Romanesque brickwork of a nearby tower, or the polychrome tiled niche on the brown brick upper storeys

Seagram Building or Working Men's Club

of a stepped pre-war high-rise. As a consequence, it does all feel like one vast anonymous surrealist artwork, where the architectural id lurks in the places where you're not meant to be looking. The San Remo Towers resemble the

A collection of Water Towers

sort of gee-gaws that were placed at the top of Stalin's post-war seven skyscrapers in Moscow, but unlike the Soviet buildings, these were not treated as objects in the round, but have a front/back relationship much as would a Victorian terrace or a Wilhelmine tenement. They are also really fucking tall, so you're constantly presented with ten, twenty, thirty storeys of bare engineering brick and spindly escape staircases overlooking streets of four-storey tenements. So San Remo Towers, for instance, is a noble

Rose Window in the Sky

stone edifice to Central Park, and a giant gasworks to the streets behind it.

Buildings like these reveal the truth in an apparently surreal line in Television's "Venus": "Broadway looked so medieval". This is a landscape which by European standards

Charlemagne with Steel Frames

Planned Accidents of the New York Zoning Code

is recent, modern, but so antiquated in its design and sometimes its technology (was the plumbing in early-twentieth-century New York really so primitive it needed all these rooftop tanks?) that it evokes New Yorker Lewis

Gimbel's Skybridge

Mumford's derisive term for the society thrown up by the first machine age — "Paleotechnical". It took a giant leap into the future with its technology (in 1923, New York already had more skyscrapers than London, the most

Back Ends of San Remo

skyscraper-filled European city, does today) but carried all the old medieval values with it. Its architecture is littered with tat from the past, placed in the most unexpected corners. In doing things first, New York's architects took excess baggage with them that more fearless emigrants would jettison. This is what European Modernists hated about New York — the disappointment that Gropius and Corbusier and Mendelsohn and Mayakovsky all felt as that steel skyline came into focus, and you could see all the trash of the old world had been nailed to the frames.[11] At this distance, it makes Manhattan a fascinating, compelling place to walk, because hardly anywhere has ever combined being quite so backwards with being quite so futuristic; the stylistic schizophrenia befits this European *tabula rasa* on the charred, cleared, redeveloped and reclaimed ruins of what the Lenape called *Manaháhtaan*, "the place for gathering wood for bows".

At the centre of all this is Grand Central Station, both an example of Beaux Arts kitsch — the iconography all around mostly refers to nothing more interesting than the Vanderbilt family, the financiers of this and much else in early-twentieth-century New York — and an exemplar of an architecture of pure space. When you're in past the accoutrements that a load of hired Parisian designers added to Reed & Stem's 1913 building to add a *touch of class*, you're in a clerestory-lit hall of great purity, both in constant motion and impossibly calm. Anything too messy, including the trains themselves, got placed underground, so that you do in fact have to scuttle down into a basement out of this magnificent showpiece if you want to actually take a train, but the effect is so impressive that I can't imagine anybody exchanging it for a more rational terminus — as was proposed on multiple occasions, until the building was listed in 1967. The closest thing to demolition was the construction of the air-rights PanAm (now MetLife) building above it, a long hated and now presumably fashionably "mid-century modern" precast concrete edifice. It was partly designed by Walter Gropius, helping to destroy the Bauhaus director's reputation in the process. But again, it was not the professedly modern buildings that really caught my extremely European eye here, but these stone-clad, pompous, ungainly monsters that give Midtown Manhattan a sense of vast age, a place whose values are already barely comprehensible. Nowhere is this more obviously the case than in the preposterous and wonderful Rockefeller Center.

Rockefeller Center was a private project, and also Manhattan's major monument to the New Deal, the class compromise that the USA had instead of (if somewhat approximating to) social democracy. At the end of the 1920s, New York inadvertently invented the "skyscraper index", which predicts that the completion of a "world's tallest" building will either immediately precede or coincide with a financial crash — under construction, the Chrysler and the Empire State Buildings added extra floors and spires to beat each other to the title, and then stood empty as the

Vanderbilt Hall, Grand Central

Great Depression collapsed the USA's unplanned, *laissez-faire* capitalism. Both the Empire State and the Chrysler are, while we're here, absolutely thrilling works of architecture, capturing the exact moment the Paleotechnic style started to become more rationalist and sober, without ever losing that sense of the bizarre and spectacular; Rockefeller Center continues in this vein. The team of architects, headed by Raymond Hood, have dropped the cupolas, Romanesque arches and Gothic tracery of earlier skyscrapers; but the buildings are still clad in stone and the windows are arranged in a rush of upward strips, rather than laid horizontally along the line of their underlying steel frames. Constructed over the course of the Depression, it was the personal project of one megacapitalist out to make a ton of money, and it was an ideological project, showcasing social peace, class collaboration and the American Way in a very conscious fashion.

In terms of its scale and its financing, Rockefeller Center is an example of what Jane Jacobs, in one of her more useful phrases, called, in *The Death and Life of Great American Cities*, "catastrophic money". It is a city within a city, a proto-megastructure, a series of interconnected skyscrapers, public buildings and theatres that takes up several blocks of Midtown Manhattan, but oddly it escaped Jacobs' ire — in her own explanation, because it actually continued rather than broke up the existing street plan. You may, in going to Rockefeller Center, pass from the ordinary streets into a privately owned, privately patrolled piece of corporate city, but you do so along the old thoroughfares. Certainly, in terms of street activity, this is correct, and the zoning is much less monofunctional than Lincoln Center; it remains a slice of Koolhaas' *Delirious New York*, with congestion and multifunctionality being encouraged; but it is surely all too nakedly capitalistic and top-down to be fully assimilated into the New York Ideology. It may *have*

Financial Crash Runner-Up — Chrysler

streets, but it does not *come from* the street. In the days of Moses, this was already "building like Moses with Jane Jacobs in mind", as Mayor Michael Bloomberg would put it in the 2000s. And Lincoln Center doesn't have an ice rink.

Financial Crash Winner — Empire

Before walking Rockefeller Center, we could pause to have a look at an account of how it came into being — that is, through another mammoth project of slum clearance. One popular tourist brochure of the time began with a photograph of "a jumbled pattern of row houses", of which "two hundred and twenty nine... were demolished to make way for today's soaring towers".[12] The author reminds visitors that Rockefeller Center was built at the height of the Great Depression, when millions were unemployed in the USA — with no social safety net — and NYC's traditional industries like textiles were hit especially hard. The *News on the March* tone continues:

> the achievement is even more impressive when one considers its timing. This inspiring demonstration of American vitality, courage, and resourcefulness came at a crucial and reassuring moment in our lives. The man on the sidewalk gazed spellbound at these soaring, confident prophets of a new era, and felt better.[13]

Unless you were one of those photogenic construction workers erecting the thing, how it was that this achievement would actually benefit *you* might have been unclear, but the buildings were keen to communicate the public benefit in a manner that was far from abstract. In 1929, John D. Rockefeller Jr had embarked upon what was billed as "the world's largest private building project",[14] and decided to continue with it despite the Depression, cushioned by his immense wealth. The management on the ground was entrusted to the young Nelson Rockefeller, who also commissioned a programme of applied art, based on the heart-swellingly American theme of "New Frontiers". These were subdivided into "Man's Progress toward Civilisation", "Man's Development in Mind and Spirit", "Man's Development in Physical and Scientific Areas" and "Man's Development of Industry and the Character of the Nation" — (note all those capitalisations), and placed the philosopher Hartley Burr Alexander in charge of assembling these *objets d'art*.

Skyscraper as Anti-Depressant

Look up, and you'll find the buildings all in the same stone and strip window vein, often with dramatically treated step-down/set-back profiles to dramatise the New York Zoning Code and in order not to cast the public spaces into darkness; but on the street, there is an enormous amount of *stuff* to look at. There are the advertisements of the Radio City Music Hall, which on the day I walked around the Center had the hysterically NYC double-bill of Tony Bennett and Lady Gaga, and there are the artworks Nelson Rockefeller dotted everywhere. At Radio City Music Hall itself, the medallion "Dance, Drama and Song" by one Hildreth M. Meière tells you some more about what you'll find inside. Nearby is a Blakean deity representing "Wisdom" by Lee Lawrie, of 1933; according to one guide, "his left hand shoves away the billowing clouds of ignorance which might obscure wisdom".[15] Lee Friedlander's "Radio" (1934), at the base of the NBC headquarters, has a clustered high relief group of voluptuously-buttocked men representing the process of communication. A coal miner and a black Caribbean plantation worker can be found carved in gold at the entrance to the British Empire Building (the British government being one of Rockefeller's many tenants); something more allegorical represents the friendship of the USA and the French Republic at the outrageously opulent, kitsch entrance to the Maison Française. The two themed buildings are separated by a "channel". The sculptures are seldom Great Art, but they are great *applied* art, in a similar vein to the artworks of the Moscow or Kyiv Metro. They tell you more about the time and its values than any masterpiece. Only one really major artist did any work here, the sculptor Isamu Noguchi, and he's here represented by a very uncharacteristic figurative group, titled simply "News". It is hilarious and brilliant, a cluster of floating hardboiled figures in stainless steel bursting out of the entrance to the Associated Press Building.

Together at Last

High-relief figures by Gaston Lachaise — a sculptor much more comfortable working on personal, highly sexualised nudes than all this improving rhetorical stuff — represent "The Gifts of Earth" and "The Spirit of Progress", framed, again, in gold. These are apparently "a reference to the bond between capitalism and the unions during the building of the Center".[16] The same sculptor was responsible for the hulking construction workers above the Brasserie, created in 1935 "To Commemorate the Workmen of the Center" — in one panel the New York proletariat can be seen breaking up a Greek column to symbolise the destruction of the old buildings on the site. The sculptural programme of Rockefeller Center, contemporary as it was with Nazism, fascism and Stalinism, has often been linked to the applied art of the dictatorships, including by Susan Sontag, who compared Lee Lawrie's brawny Atlas, the Center's largest artwork, to "the bronze colossi of Arno Breker" in her extremely NYC essay on "Fascinating Fascism".[17] The similarities are obvious enough, though architecturally, it's far less fascistic than the mini-EUR of Lincoln Center. The sculptures are more ostentatiously sexy and silly than what you would get in the average totalitarian state, but the more interesting discussion might be about the way in which they engage in the New Deal's project of class reconciliation.

The most important artwork Nelson Rockefeller commissioned for the Center stands now in Mexico City. That is, Diego Rivera's mural of "Man at the Crossroads", which partakes of the same representational, big-subjects, big-use-of-the-term-"Man" programme as everything else, but was destroyed at the request of the Rockefeller family due to its prominent inclusion of Lenin in the composition; Rivera reconstructed the work at the Palace of Fine Arts in the Mexican capital. Ironically enough, explicitly fascist bas-reliefs at the Center's Palazzo d'Italia were left alone

43

Allegory of Britain

until the war. Much in the sculptural programme resembles both the burly symbolic nudes of Italian fascist public sculpture and the heroic, active proletarians of Socialist Realism (much more than the terrifyingly dead-eyed and stiff pseudo-Greek sculpture popular in Nazi Germany), and while it celebrates "the worker", it keeps that very abstract, with no discernible relation to the more fallible bodies

Allegory of France

of any actually existing working person. But, there is no personal glorification of the Rockefellers (as the Vanderbilts

NEWS!!!

were glorified at Grand Central), and the accessibility of the complex is a statement of would-be-democratic openness. Like Marshall Berman's mum at Times Square, you can go and "bathe" in it all and nobody will stop you, even despite there being nothing much you can do without paying for it, bar just looking.

Jacobs' approval of Rockefeller Center shows that "projects" were sometimes OK, if they obeyed certain planning principles. One of the more interesting exponents of the New York Ideology was less forgiving. In *The Assassination of New York*, Robert Fitch developed the notion of the Rockefellers as purveyors of "catastrophic money". The original Center was a financial failure (it did not make a profit until the 1960s), and so the family kept constructing more office space around it to try and recentre the city around their investment, and in the process gradually helped destroy the diversified economy of what was once an industrial city, reshaping Manhattan into an immense office complex. It's often forgotten by we tourists that the Depression-era buildings are just one part of Rockefeller Center, just a sliver of the family's parcel of Midtown. Rockefeller Center kept getting built well into the 1970s, with increasingly Miesesque repeated facades by Wallace K. Harrison replacing Raymond Hood's more romantic towers and squares; they can be seen from the earlier buildings in *enfilade*, like the townscape of Jacques Tati's *Playtime*. They no longer successfully convince the pedestrian that he or she is benefitting in some manner from their construction. But I wasn't deterred. As a townscape Midtown is on such a dementedly heroic scale that, like Berman, you can tie yourself up in knots trying to explain how this thing which is aimed against everything you believe in is actually a fulfilment of it. Certainly by the point I left the Center and walked in the direction of Downtown, I had temporarily ceased being an English smartarse and given myself entirely to the cityscape. At one point, I found myself without thinking literally skipping down Broadway.

Playtime for Nelson Rockefeller

Even then, Greenwich Village was not for me — like the Modernist skyscrapers, the Georgian streets are nice to have if you live here, but if you don't, they are done much better elsewhere; to go from London across the Atlantic to look at classical redbrick terraces seems like a drastic category error. I did pause in Mercer Street Books, and came out with two paperbacks that would prove to be useful in understanding the city — Laura Rosen's *Top of the City*, a book about these bizarre gimcrack steampunk rooftops, and Benjamin Davis's *Communist Councilman from Harlem*, the autobiography, written in a federal prison, of one of NYC's two Communist elected representatives in the CPUSA's pre-McCarthy glory years. I noted that Washington Square really is genuinely filled with people hanging out playing music and dancing, confirming the wisdom of not building a freeway underneath it, and admired I. M. Pei's Jacobs-antagonising Brutalist halls of residence for New York University, looming over the preserved early-nineteenth-century townscape of the Village like a shadow of what might have been if the Lower Manhattan Expressway had actually been built.

Village Voices

Another Greenwich Village

Deeper into Downtown, things get Paleotechnical again, though in a slightly more familiar way to the British observer — the cast-iron and brick warehouses are evocative of Manchester around Whitworth Street, or of Glasgow's Merchant City, high-tech buildings with high windows and enough Neoclassical or Neo-Gothic trimmings to distract pedestrians from their otherwise clear and proud mechanical modernity. I was here to look for Louis Sullivan's Bayard Building. This was my first and for all I knew last time in the Great Satan, and as I might never get to Chicago, I made sure I had a taste of "Chicago School" proto-Modernism in NYC. Sullivan is one of those figures who lost the battle in their lifetime but won a war for their posthumous reputation, created and inflated in large part by his apprentice Frank Lloyd Wright. In the 1880s, Sullivan was one of several Chicago architects who tried to develop that new invention, the skyscraper, into a raw and novel American architecture, rather than a stacked-up emulation of Old Europe. A dozen or so buildings along these lines were erected in the new mid-Western industrial city, but there is just the one here. Sullivan was unimpressed by New York, writing in his pompous, Whitmanian, third-person *Autobiography of an Idea* (sample chapter title: "Louis Goeth on a Journey") that its architects had even less taste than those of Chicago, despite the city's greater age. Manhattan displayed "a singularly sordid, vulgar vernacular of architectural speech... the only difference he could see between the vernacular of the East and that of the West was that one was older and staler".[18] After the Bayard Building, a twelve-storey office block for the Union Loan and Investment Company, Sullivan was not asked back.[19]

The Bayard Building is small by today's standards, but perhaps a skyscraper by the standards of 1898, when it was completed. It follows Sullivan's precepts in his 1896 essay on "The Tall Office Building Artistically Considered": that a skyscraper should have a base, a shaft and a capital, like a Classical column, and that its decoration should be treated accordingly, rather than as a collection of "quotations" and scholarly references. In New York it is evident this essay was

A Tall Office Building Artistically Considered

roundly ignored until the end of the 1920s, with the grimly, queasily fascinating results that we've already discussed; but Sullivan's alternative to forty-storey baroque tenements was not as simplistic as his posthumous reception might suggest. Sullivan coined the term "form follows function", but he had a very particular idea of what "following" meant in this context. The "shaft" of the Bayard Building is a grid of glass and terracotta panels, divided by delicate, thin mullions, repetitious and mechanised, in a way that clearly tells you, "I am a large tall building held up by a steel frame". But the base and the capital are obsessively decorative, in an original, personal variant of Art Nouveau; a series of identical angels, wings outspread, look down from the top floor, and on the ground, a cobwebby skein of vegetal and vaginal motifs meet the curious pedestrian.

That all this was irrelevant for roughly the next forty years is made clear enough when you walk from here to take a look around some of the famous pre-Modernist skyscrapers of Downtown. The Neo-Gothic Woolworth Building is the most famous, designed by Cass Gilbert in 1911, opened two years later. It had been constructed in

Form, following Function

record time; by comparison, the Palace of Westminster, completed in 1870, with its tall but comparatively diminutive clocktower, took thirty years to build. The Woolworth was the tallest building in the world for a couple of decades, and Sullivan would surely have found its ornament pretentious and derivative. Anyone who believed in the principles of Gothic architecture would have been horrified to see how, here, production-line crockets were turned out as if on a lathe and then nailed to a steel frame — but, it recognises, as something like the Ansonia does not, that a very tall building needs an upwards momentum: and so all the Gothic tat here is swept up into a single, moronic and inexorable upwards momentum, as simple and irresistible as a Ramones song — 1, 2, 3, 4! But while the Woolworth Building is usually pegged as the inspiration for Stalin's Moscow skyscrapers, the more likely candidate is the nearby Municipal Building, a 1914 design by McKim, Mead and White right on the edge of Manhattan island. As in Moscow, the actual ornament is Classical rather than Gothic, and the spreading wings of the complex feel authentically Muscovite, an entire complex rather than a tower. Again, there is an obvious base/shaft/capital divide, but this is so much more sinister than anything Sullivan put his hand to — a cynical, conservative architecture, powerful in the manner of a Vanderbilt or a Rockefeller.

In the area around, things get more sinister still. Incredibly to a European, some of New York's notoriously fearsome prisons are in inner-urban skyscrapers, among them the complex known as "the Tombs", adjacent to the Municipal Building, and like it a showcase of what American state power actually meant at the time for many people. The skyscraper part of the Tombs is the Manhattan Detention Complex, designed in the Thirties by Harvey Wiley Corbett, an architect otherwise best known for his drawings of a futuristic steampunk Manhattan of skybridges and flying

The original Cathedral of Commerce

cars; and a skybridge does indeed connect it to the adjacent Criminal Court, a melodramatic "Bridge of Sighs", evocative and in very macabre taste. Today, the majority of the prison accommodation is in a thuggish, slit-windowed, concrete

Municipal Proto-Stalinism

high-rise, designed by Urbahn Associates and receiving its
first inmates in 1989. At that time, Brutalist buildings were
still acceptable as long as they were designed specifically for

The Tombs, and its "Bridge of Sighs"

punishment. Here, you realise, is a country that really likes prisons.

On my way back to the Upper West, as it got too dark for printable photographs, I detoured into Battery Park

Carceral Brutalism

City, another massive "project". This one is of interest to Londoners as the direct blueprint for Canary Wharf. The same structure, under the control of a development quango unanswerable to local government (in this case, New York

Calatrava's PATH Station

State's Urban Development Corporation (UDC)); the same dockside location; the same chain-store blandness; the same developer, the Canadian conglomerate Olympia and York; and the same architecture, only here there were several Cesar Pelli towers rather than one, and some have domes rather than pyramids at their apex. By then, that was enough for one day.

I had enjoyed myself immensely on this extremely long walk. I was exhausted (I realised later I had walked around seven miles; it remains the longest walk I have ever taken, and until winding up at the depressing Battery Park, I barely felt it) and I now understood something of what it is people like about this place — spectacle, grandeur, the bizarre. But there was also no doubt that the city I had seen up to this point supported the familiar story of New York's apparent whitewashing and gentrification. It looked

overwhelmingly rich, only a little less overwhelmingly
white, and very heavily policed. I was told by a security
guard (politely — "Sir, excuse me, Sir") not to photograph
the Woolworth Building up close; and of course, what used
to be the World Trade Center is at the heart of Downtown. It
is not rewarding to explore. Nearly all the new architecture
I had seen on my walk was awful, from the overbearing
digital trash of Thom Mayne's complex for Cooper Union
to the horribly bland, committee-designed blue-glass
replacement skyscrapers for the destroyed World Trade
Center itself. The only building designed after the Seventies
I rather admired was Santiago Calatrava's PATH Station
for the commuter rail link from the WTC to New Jersey,
then still under construction. It is a project which went
massively overbudget — to $4 billion — and was heavily
criticised for it in a city where Subway stations are mostly
coated in filth. It is at least spacious and attractive for a
public purpose.[20] Around a tenth of its budget could have
built an entire Metro system in China or Spain.

Walk 2
Maps and Conduits

On subsequent days I caught some glimpses of another city. Before the lecture at Columbia University, which was my actual reason for being here, I crossed Central Park, marvelling again at its proto-Stalinist apartment towers, to the two big Modernist museums on the Upper East Side: the cylinder of Frank Lloyd Wright's Guggenheim and the angular, cantilevered cube of Marcel Breuer's (then-closed) Whitney. Both are powerful architecture, but caught rather incongruously in streets upon streets of Neo-Baroque villas and luxury flats, making them into stand-alone sculptural objects, baubles — but undoubtedly, for all their abstraction, not *projects* (and my camera then ran out of battery; idiotically, I did not pack a charger, and so the rest of this walk is illustrated by photographs kindly contributed by Samuel Medina). After the lecture, I was taken out for dinner in Harlem. Walking along 125th street to the Subway, past the Apollo — *the* Apollo! — and the ordinary, somewhat rubbish-strewn street of ordinary chain stores was redolent of nowhere more dramatic than Lewisham. From here, I also experienced some further quirks of the Subway.

What now exists was once three separate systems, two private and one municipal, which were nationalised and placed under the city's control in 1940, under the left-liberal mayorship of Fiorello La Guardia. The private companies' names ("the IRT", etc) are, like the District and

Wright's Manhattan Spiral

Metropolitan in London, still used for their old lines. But this wasn't what was confusing. The amount of express trains (rare on the tube — only the Metropolitan has them) can ambush the unprepared, and took me a fair few stops

Impromptu Commerce outside the Whitney

past where I wanted to be; but more offensive was the mindboggling map. New York has the most extensive metro in the world — an achievement, to be sure — and a flat fare encouraging exploration beyond the daily commute. Yet it has decided, in the Metropolitan Transit Authority's (MTA) infinite wisdom, to have a nearly exactly realistic rather than schematic map, featuring the actual streets and landmarks beneath the coloured subway lines. In an act of hilarious pedantry, the map-makers have rendered every curve in the lines as they cross the river from Manhattan into Brooklyn, on the grounds, apparently, that people would otherwise be confused if their train leant somewhat as it passed under the East River. It is astoundingly irritating to anybody who doesn't live here, and in its creation lies a tale.

In 1972, the newly founded MTA unveiled a striking, colourful new map to the Subway, created under the direction of the Italian designer Massimo Vignelli, who also then created the colour-coding system and the Helvetica signs that distinguish the system. The new map followed, and elaborated on the model of transport map used in much of the world, introduced first in London during the 1930s by the engineering draughtsman Harry Beck, inspired by the diagrams of electrical circuits. When underground, Beck argued, you didn't need to know where you were. You needed to get where you were going. For that you needed absolute clarity, with nothing superfluous — a Modernist ethos then being rolled out across London Transport's stations, posters and signs. The result, an abstract diagram whose only geographical feature was a stylised river Thames, was so successful that within a couple of decades, most big cities in the world copied Beck. New York first introduced a Beck-style map in 1967, but did so at the same time that several lines were reorganised and rebranded. It confused New Yorkers so much it caused public consternation and even a train going in the wrong direction. This chaos led to the creation of the MTA in 1968, with a mandate to finally sort the system out. In 1972, a new map was unveiled. It was a product of Massimo Vignelli's company Unimark, its lead designer being Joan Charysyn. She took Vignelli's instruction to "draw spaghetti lines" and ran with it, using vivid artificial colours. The result was a curvaceous Pop Art design classic. The MTA even made a tidy sum selling T-shirts and posters with Vignelli and Charasyn's map on it. You see it around, still, in New York, sometimes as an alternative "Subway diagram" — though you won't find it in subway trains, where it would be most useful.

The Subway fell into sharp decline in the 1970s, like much else in the city; Vignelli and Charysyn had to update the map nearly every year to remove lines that had been closed. The Subway, now graffiti-caked, became known as a place of crime and anomie, of man being beast to man.

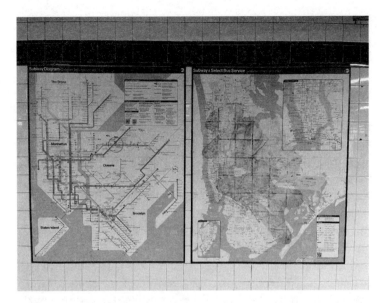

Public Comment on the rival Maps (SM)

As design historian Peter Lloyd notes in his book on the Vignelli map, those who raged against the abstract grid made their case by appealing to "human nature". New Yorkers didn't want to go to Subway stations, they said — they wanted to go to "places".[1] The map took all the incomprehensible vitality of New York and tried to make it simple and understandable — that is, it tried to treat New York City like a *project*. According to John Tauranac, the MTA employee responsible for the ridiculous current map, people didn't *want* simplicity, and they certainly didn't want Modernism. They wanted to know where they really were, in real space. These ideas were in the air at the time; a particular version of the neoliberal notion that human behaviour could never be planned and truly understood, and hence that planning was inherently foolish. The administrators of a public transit system should not expect such irrational, intuitive and impulsive animals to be able to understand a network through an abstract diagram. They should be given a representation of what there really is and then left alone. And yet, every other big city in the world manages it just fine.

So after getting the wrong trains for an hour or so, I made it back to my hotel in the Upper West, and planned a last day's walk. I concentrated on Lower Manhattan, as I had an appointment in Wall Street — I would go to the High Line before, and Brooklyn Bridge after it. I was dazzled, rapt by the High Line, as unconflictedly excited by it as I was by Broadway and Rockefeller Center. The converted overhead railway begins in Chelsea, an uninteresting district with an interesting history, similar culturally, geographically and architecturally to Shoreditch; it runs from there to the back end of Penn Station, for a couple of miles in total. It was criticised by the more literal-minded Jacobsians, with a particularly shrill condemnation from one of her more conservative disciples, the New Urbanist James Howard Kunstler, who seemed particularly offended by the idea of a street running in the air — exactly what Saint Jane said you shouldn't do! This thing isn't even a street! It has no Bodegas! But it is as filled with people as Broadway, somehow unperturbed by the fact that they're strolling, promenading, at third-or-fourth-storey level. In fact, the High Line is a very belated fulfilment of those steampunk dreams of a New York of streets in the air, carved, appropriately, out of a surviving industrial remnant of its pre-war Gilded Age.

The High Line is, however, a perfect example of the necessity for being careful what you wish for; it was preserved after decades of battles by campaigners, the same people who were found in the Eighties and Nineties resisting the gentrification of the industrial corners of Manhattan, and the replacement of lively, repurposed spaces with rubbish like Battery Park City. When the viaduct was eventually restored, the redesign by Diller, Scofidio and Renfro was exquisitely tasteful. I found the most to admire in the landscaping by James Corner Field Operations, thickets of tall wild grasses that evoked an only slightly tamed version of what grew here during the line's years of dereliction. It is also a fabulous way of seeing swathes of western Manhattan's stranger architecture, one outlandish monument after another — the forbidding, cliff-like Neo-Georgian apartment complex of London Terrace, a gargantuan Dolphin Square; the thrilling steamline moderne factory complex of the Starrett-Lehigh Building; the serried towers-in-a-park of Penn South; and finally, Davis, Brody and Associates' Westyard Distribution Center, a ziggurat-like, concrete megastructure that surmounts the lines into Penn Station, with row upon row of silvery Amtrak trains being fed into its Moloch-like maw.[2] It is also, very obviously, a machine for generating gentrification and overdevelopment. Everything around it became suddenly more expensive — hotels and condos and office blocks sprouted around its off-ramps and steps, and the high-rise Standard Hotel by Ennead Architects was actually built on top of it. It's surprisingly very fine, one of the best new buildings I saw in Manhattan: torqued into two glass wings and hauled up on pilotis, like a Corbusier or Niemeyer building.

Manfredo Tafuri wrote that New York's Paleotechnical skyscrapers were best conceived not as architecture, but as "real live bombs with chain effects, designed to explode the real-estate market... an instrument — and no longer an 'expression' — of economic policy".[3] The way the city was laid out encouraged and complemented this process. The combination of the steel frame, the grid plan and the wealth of American agriculture and industry at the turn of the century all came together to create a new

Apparently this is a London Terrace (SM)

kind of infrastructure, one based on making money first and architecture much later. The High Line, while totally different in its conception and history, is infrastructure with a similar effect — a conduit for stimulating property

The Starrett-Lehigh Building seen from the High Line (SM)

development with devastating effectiveness. Like the old skyscrapers or Rockefeller Center (but unlike the blander Battery Park City) it offers so much visual excitement, so much of the unexpected, so much street life and activity, that it appears as a generous, public-spirited endeavour; but this is a side-effect. The High Line *appears* as marvellously public and untamed, at least until you find the long list of things you can't do there, like listen to amplified music or organise a protest.

Wall Street, on the other hand, was not quite the festival of money I had expected. Visiting the headquarters of a left-wing book publisher in one of those Baroque skyscrapers, I was told that it was actually fairly cheap to rent an office there — many of the financial institutions had moved over the Hudson to Jersey City, a little thicket of new glass skyscrapers facing Battery Park City, where a "Wall Street West" was built amidst the panic and paranoia after the September 11 atrocity. From Wall Street I walked to Brooklyn Bridge, which is as people say it is, but it was something I saw on the way that really crystallised what had confused me in Manhattan. Usually, I make a point of going to look at social housing on a visit to a city like this. There is usually some complex, some sort of famous monument — a Trellick Tower, a Brunswick Centre, a Habitat 67, a Karl-Marx-Hof or Karl-Marx-Allee — where you can see how housing needs were or were intended to be provided in the twentieth century by the social democratic state. I didn't know what this might be in Manhattan, but what I found instead was puzzling indeed.

I was in the Lower East Side, specifically a district called Two Bridges, named after the Brooklyn and Manhattan, whose immense pylons bisect the area. Most of it was made up of what we would describe as "council estates" — publicly-owned housing rented from the local government (here, the New York City Housing Authority (NYCHA)), built

Admiring The Standard Hotel (SM)

in the mid-twentieth century. The basics were familiar —
affordable flats, laid out following planning principles that
emphasised access to light, air and greenery over closeness
to high streets and workplaces — but aesthetically, this

was harsh, to put it mildly. I was looking at Alfred E. Smith Houses, built between 1950 and 1953, and named after the progressive New York State governor who passed the laws in the Twenties that allowed New York to construct public housing.

A British council estate of the same period will have large windows, a mix of low and high-rise housing, carefully considered surface materials — different colours of brick or shuttered concrete, and balconies, and all of that in a bankrupt country whose cities were emerging from six years of aerial bombing. But here, everything was covered in one brick, in one colour. The frontages of the buildings were totally flat; there were no balconies, and most obviously of all, only the most minuscule windows. Yet it was extraordinary to see this place still surviving, given just how gentrified was the city I had seen up to that point. This was also, for the first time, a place I'd seen here that wasn't mainly white. This is part of Chinatown, and most of the tenants in the towers here are East Asian. They live here in decent, if unattractive housing on a site which could be sold for enough money to buy several entire islands. But to see something so harsh and so dour on such an astonishing site — between Brooklyn Bridge and Manhattan Bridge, with a view of two rivers and the Statue of Liberty and the Downtown skyline — was bracing, especially given those tiny windows. Were people not meant to look at the view?

Reading up on this later, it was unsurprising to find that this was the direct result of the regulations underpinning public housing in the US. Its construction, which began slowly in the Twenties, was given new impetus and federal funding in the 1937 Wagner-Steagall Act. President Truman's Housing Act of 1949 cemented state backing for public housing as part of "slum clearance". But the overwhelming emphasis of the Roosevelt and Truman governments was on private housing, underwritten but not

Public Spaces of the Alfred E. Smith Houses (SM)

directly built by the state, via subsidised mortgages from the new Federal Housing Agency and a publicly-funded highway network, creating the new low-rise suburbs that spread around each American city. While Britain after 1945 was trying to move away from the "ribbon development" it had favoured in the inter-war years, the US gave suburbia a new shot of life. While public housing was built in larger numbers as a result of both acts, they added an income ceiling for tenants, a requirement that public housing be *solely* for the poor. The 1937 Act also stipulated public housing be built to lower standards so it wasn't "unfair competition" with the market product. In Britain, meanwhile, a Victorian requirement that public housing be solely for "the working classes" was removed by the 1945 Labour government, so it could be for everyone. So when, in 1961 James Baldwin walked around a Harlem under reconstruction, and found that "the projects are hideous... there being a law, apparently respected throughout the world, that popular housing shall be as cheerless as a prison",[4] he was factually wrong only insofar as there was indeed such a law — but only in the USA.

Walk 3
The Welfare Island

I came back to New York eight years later, in a July heatwave: though the freakish geophysics of global warming meant that at 35 degrees centigrade it was actually cooler than an unbearable 40 degrees in London. It was my first long-distance journey since the start of the COVID-19 pandemic, and masks had only just been phased out as compulsory on transatlantic flights. I was *extremely nervous*. But while JFK was as nasty as before — perhaps just a little more so, in fact — I had planned the rest of the journey to be different. I knew I hadn't even begun to get under the skin of New York. I had seen a visually dramatic but comprehensively gentrified skyscraper city, almost ancient in its appearance, and I knew this couldn't be anything like the whole story. So I would stay for eight days, billeted in a hotel in the South Bronx, once the devastated epicentre of New York's 1970s disaster decade. When I mentioned where I would be staying to an English friend, long resident in NYC, he sent me a link to a development of luxury apartment towers under construction in said district, evidently keen to divest me of any notion there was any way out.

In the nearly ten years since I last visited, I had been reading a lot about New York. An ageing socialist from the city stood for the Democratic nomination in 2016 and nearly won. Although he was smashed, unexpectedly, by a barely *compos mentis* Joe Biden in 2020, in his wake a much younger generation of socialists, mostly members of the Democratic Socialists of America (DSA) — a loosely-organised organisation that derives at several removes from one of the many splits in the old Socialist Party of America — were elected to local councils, legislatures and the House of Representatives in Washington. Despite some setbacks, Sanders and the DSA have not faced the humiliation their British counterparts, Jeremy Corbyn and Momentum, have been subjected to since 2019; rather, the Biden administration has deployed the riskier but more insidious technique of co-option rather than destruction of the new left. Proportionally, the largest number of the young socialist officials in recent years have been elected in New York; the shift began when two socialist activists, Alexandria Ocasio-Cortez and Jamaal Bowman, scalped long-serving centrists in Congress seats spanning the Bronx and Queens.[1] The DSA is now the biggest socialist organisation in the USA for a century, nearly the largest in its history: it has an estimated 80,000 members, close to the 100,000 members the Socialist Party of America had before it was destroyed in the post-WW1 Red Scare, and a little more than the 70,000 dues-paying members the Communist Party USA had at its WW2 peak. Not coincidentally, there has been a huge amount of revisionist literature on socialism and the USA in recent years, some of it focusing on New York as the centre of a bygone American socialism.

There was another way of seeing the city. You did not, unlike Marshall Berman, need to invoke the dialectic to explain why Marxists should love Disney and Nasdaq: it turned out that New York once built public housing and housing co-operatives and municipal hospitals, and you could love them, too. Moreover, the story of how these emerged in the Thirties and were crushed during the Seventies was of relevance to young socialists interested in power. Forgotten books were rediscovered, like

76

Vivian Gornick's extraordinary *The Romance of American Communism*; but there were also new books that placed the New York Ideology in significant doubt. Kim Phillips-Fein's *Fear City* charted how the city's banks manufactured a crisis in the 1970s to smash to pieces what they regarded as a social democratic cuckoo in the nest; Lizabeth Cohen's *Saving America's Cities* hailed the achievements one of the city's major statist planners and a leading member of Jane Jacobs' shitlist, Ed Logue, the chair of the New York State Urban Development Corporation; the collectively written volume *Affordable Housing in New York* argued that NYC was actually one of the great world cities for social housing, and described dozens of examples to prove it. There were even a couple of books that tried to salvage the reputation of Robert Moses. I read most of these, some of them on the plane, to prime me for seeing a different city this time. I also consulted a contemporary witness: the Works' Progress Administration's series of *WPA Guides*, an incredible wealth of information on the USA circa 1938 at the height of the New Deal, funded by the government and compiled by the employees of the Federal Writers' Project, illustrated with everything from Pictorialist photographs to Expressionist woodcuts.

What I saw first, on a jetlagged journey to Manhattan to undertake the paid work I was ostensibly here for, was a capitalist city that had become only more melodramatically unequal. Looking south in Central Park, you can see half-a-dozen pencil towers all along 57th Street, super-tall skyscrapers that are each around an apartment wide; they have a chilling abstraction that makes them far more interesting to look at than the dull, cheap-looking towers that replaced the destroyed World Trade Center. The idea is startlingly, brutally simple, one floor to one plutocrat, each with the most minimal architectural expression possible, stacked as tall as they can possibly get without falling over.[2] What they represent is abominable, and many of the higher flats are so battered by the wind that they are apparently barely inhabitable. These towers are the ultimate architectural status-objects, and, visible on any

New Obelisks of Very Late Capitalism

raised ground in all five boroughs, they may have helped to make a new generation of socialists.

After this, I went first to a place I had been recommended in 2014 by a young architecture critic — Roosevelt Island. This is a thin little island between Manhattan and Queens that had been redeveloped over the 1970s by the New York State Urban Development Corporation (UDC) into a mammoth social housing complex, and one of New York's rare examples of social Brutalism. The Subway ride that takes you there is a surprise too, spitting you out of the walk-down, low-ceilinged, grime-caked cut-and-cover network built between the 1900s and 1930s into a spacious, deep-level concrete and tile hall, with a red-painted space frame above. You could for a moment be somewhere with attractive public transport, a Vienna or a Montreal. On leaving the station, you have a fascinating panorama of Manhattan, full of unexpected things.

Wedged in between Art Deco and mock-Tudor luxury flats is a magnificent frontal view of the United Nations Secretariat Building, designed by Wallace K. Harrison in 1947, from a slab-block curtain wall idea developed, according to his own account, by Le Corbusier. The UN HQ was praised/criticised in a similar way to the Seagram Building for being a break with the unplanned, street-focused Manhattan tradition — but it is a great deal more impressive today, in part simply because there is nothing nearby copying it. In the sun, framed by trees and the East River, its gleaming grid of glass, encased in its walls of white marble, is unexpectedly pure and glorious. On the other side of the steel thickets of the high-level Queensboro Bridge that crosses the island is the skyscraper tower and sprawling wings of the Cornell Medical Center, a teaching hospital praised by Lewis Mumford in the 1930s for its public purpose, its scale, repetition, and for being, for once in the city, "a unified whole".[3] Mumford lived in

Queens, in the garden suburb of Sunnyside Gardens — so a certain local pride may have entered into his claim that the hospital helped make this oblique view of Manhattan every bit as impressive as the famous panoramas of Midtown and Downtown.

Roosevelt Island would become a tourist attraction for this view, and you can sit and take it in on specially provided deckchairs; or, you can view it from cable cars which run across the East River along the Queensboro Bridge. There is a monument to Roosevelt here, too, in Four Freedoms Park (of speech; of worship; from want; from fear) making the island into New York's retrospective tribute to the New Deal moment. It was designed in the Seventies by Louis Kahn, and eventually constructed in the 2010s, using granite, rather than Kahn's favoured concrete. It is stark and hieratic, an abstract series of pylons and plinths at

Taking in the UN View

Taking in the Hospital View

the very tip of the island, looking at the Atlantic, without fences or spikes in your way, almost inviting you to swim out to sea. It is all a little pompous, with its bust of the President in the middle, though its sheer emptiness gives it a brisk freshness, in a city where so much is so closely packed. But the housing was what I was here for. Most of Roosevelt Island is dominated by one housing complex, built during the apparently disastrous Seventies by the architect and anti-fascist Catalan exile Josep Lluís Sert, to a plan by the mildly reformed American fascist Philip Johnson.[4] It is far more impressive than the public housing I had seen in Two Bridges; the centrally located Brunswick Centre I had been looking for, the housing monument that Manhattan *appears* to lack.

Tall, articulated, chunky brick and concrete blocks, with strongly expressed, heraldic concrete service towers and balconies (some of them personalised with tenants' oddments — flowers, busts, ceramic dogs) run alongside a pedestrian-only promenade, and they step down towards the Queens side of the river, creating a ziggurat-like effect,

Instead of Socialism — FDR

framed by water on both sides. Seen as an ensemble this is as dramatic and heroic in its conception as one of the socialist housing estates of New Belgrade. It is also excellent up close, with good details and an interesting and unusual relationship with the ground. On the Queens side, there are enclosed public parks, which look well maintained and homely, with some of the warm, friendly and small-scale character of the Lillington Gardens estate in Pimlico; Sert's buildings even encompass and embrace a handsome red brick church in the same manner as the London estate draws a G. E. Street church into itself. On the ground floor are shops. They are not part of a "real" NYC street — car use is strictly limited, there are few side streets, there is just the one landlord — but it is obviously street-focused, with sheltered, glazed shopping arcades running the length of the blocks, containing an encouragingly ordinary collection of groceries, community centres and cafés. This place is both heroically scaled and intimately humane, a social architecture that is properly built and maintained. It is a project, to be sure, and it is a very good one — a case for the defence of projects. It poses, in a completely different sense, the same question as the Alfred E. Smith Homes in Two Bridges. How did it happen?

Roosevelt Island, renamed as part of the UDC project, was originally Welfare Island, a place where various insanitary and infectious things were dumped in the gilded-age city; the Smallpox Hospital still stands, derelict even now and surrounded by a dense little nature reserve. Its remodelling into the place you can see today was the flagship of the UDC, the quango which later developed the considerably less interesting Battery Park City. The body was set up by the state governor, Nelson Rockefeller, in 1968. For Robert Fitch, it was yet another of that family's property development boondoggles, part of their dogged and, in his view, eventually successful attempt to transform

Drivers Must Yield

the entire centre of New York into one giant Rockefeller
Center. In the more sympathetic recent account of Lizabeth
Cohen, it was intended from the start as part of New York's
social democratic state within a state, and its opacity and

lack of democratic control was designed not as a machine for making profit, but rather as a way of getting around suburban America's suspicion of social housing. By creating an arms-length quango based on "moral obligation" bonds rather than bonds directly underwritten by the state, Nelson Rockefeller ensured that the UDC could circumvent New York state's tendency to vote down anything that involved public spending and the issuing of state bonds to build non-profit housing — something which had been defeated several times in referenda.

For Nelson Rockefeller and for Ed Logue, the Boston-born, left-liberal bureaucrat appointed to run the UDC, the model was the British New Towns, which used wholly undemocratic Development Corporations. The UDC, as Cohen describes it, was devised by Logue — as part of his conditions for taking the job — as a "'one-stop service' that could acquire project sites and then develop, finance, design, build and sell or own the resulting structures".[5] Such a level of control would ensure significant independence of the vagaries of the property market. Very soon, it all failed — the UDC's default in 1975 was one of the proximate causes of the New York fiscal crisis, by which time Rockefeller was the deputy to a president who told the city to "drop dead".[6] The UDC was remodelled by the 1980s into the Canary Wharf-anticipating, straightforwardly capitalist quango that built Battery Park City; it still exists, renamed the Empire State Development Corporation in the 1990s. It simply promotes "development", and social housing is not seen as part of that anymore.

Rockefeller created the UDC in the aftermath of the urban riots of 1968 and the rise of Black Power, evidently in the fear that actual insurrection might be possible if something wasn't done to humanise American capitalism. Roosevelt Island was notable for the fact that, like nearly all UDC schemes (other examples are Riverbend, a Brutalist estate in Harlem, and Marcus Garvey Village, a low-rise/ high-density estate by a team of later-to-be-famous architects in Brooklyn) it *didn't* involve slum clearance. This particular aspect of "urban renewal", widely criticised — evidently correctly, in the case of Lincoln Center — as being simply "negro removal", was opposed by a strong, cross-class coalition of activists by the Seventies. Instead of a housing project, the UDC described the island as a "New-Town-in-Town" (the island is *in* the Borough of Manhattan, despite not being *on* Manhattan). And for further credit where it is due, much of what makes it attractive comes from Philip Johnson's masterplan. The layouts of the buildings along the island were designed so as to give even residents whose blocks faced Queens a full view of Manhattan. Those "streets" were, Johnson stated with his usual blithe cynicism, his own version of the ideas of the most famous opponent of urban renewal: "this is my Jane Jacobs period".[7] Roosevelt Island was full of weird and progressive ideas. There were (and still are) free, battery-powered buses; cars were tamed, and actually banned from entire swathes of the island; trash was thrown out via a Swedish vacuum waste-disposal system; and given the Subway extension was going to take a while (it didn't open until 1989), connection with Manhattan was via an "aerial tram", those cable cars you can still see going alongside the Queensboro Bridge.

This first phase of Roosevelt Island was not free-market housing, but was subsidised, rent-controlled and heavily regulated. It was not, however, a *public* housing complex, no matter how much it resembled one in London or Belgrade. The finance was complicated — the UDC's bondholders naturally wanted a return on their investment — and so was the allocation of tenure. Sert's housing blocks were divided between low-income social flats, funded by the department of Housing and Urban Development (HUD) in Washington,

Roosevelt Island Gardens

middle-income flats funded by New York state's Mitchell-Lama scheme (more of which later), and co-operatives aimed at the "upper-middle income" resident. Logue was an opponent of pure public housing, which he considered to be intrinsically segregating (which, in terms of American law, it was), creating "large-scale, institutionalised apartheid projects".[8] The way his alternative was carried out could be a little shady.

Speaking when white New Yorkers were leaving for the suburbs at a rapid rate (and a couple of decades before their kids and grandkids, the "gentrifiers", would return in similarly huge numbers), Logue claimed that Roosevelt Island was "perhaps our last chance to demonstrate that people of different incomes, races and ethnic origins can live together", and, importantly, "send their children to the same public schools", such as the elegant little Modernist school on the island.[9] Logue and the UDC had a stated bias towards attracting white residents at first, as a way of ensuring the area wasn't wholly black and Hispanic during the years of white flight; the assumption, depressing if perhaps correct at the time, was that white working- and lower-middle-class New Yorkers wouldn't move to a development in which they would be a minority. Singapore- style racial quotas were instituted: there was initially a stated aim that Roosevelt Island's population should be only 30% non-white, which was slightly higher than the percentage in the city as a whole at the time it was built. Roosevelt Island in the 2020s is around 50% white, slightly higher than the percentage today in the city as a whole; this makes it unusual now in New York's non-market housing, but it remains more mixed in class terms than the luxury housing on the other sides of the river. These are on both sides now. The main monument on the Queens side is still the immense Ravenswood Power Station, but south of it you can glimpse the expensive new high-rises of Long Island City, whose model of "trickle-down" hasn't granted New Yorkers anything like the really existing affordable housing you can still see on Roosevelt Island.

Only some of the high ideals have survived, and the complex is now somewhat beleaguered. Near the station are dull, unimaginative and ultra-high-density new flats, selling at market rate. As Matthias Altwicker writes in *Affordable Housing in New York*, most of the original housing has been fully privatised, except for Eastwood, one of the largest segments of Sert's complex, containing one thousand flats; but Eastwood in turn has been bought out by developers who have housed wealthier tenants in the flats when they have been vacated. "Since 2007", Altwicker writes, "the share of below market tenants has fallen from 87 to 58 percent".[10] All this wrangling was and is ugly, and would have been impossible in a genuinely social democratic housing system, in which different races and classes can and do rent from the state. Conveniently, there is an example of pure public housing very nearby which one can look at by comparison. Its reputation precedes it.

One stop on the Subway from Roosevelt Island — a place considered so safe that a UN Secretary General, Kofi Annan, rented a flat there during his tenure — is Queensbridge Houses, the largest public housing estate in the USA. With its over three thousand flats, it is, according to the editors of *Affordable Housing in New York*, "larger than the entire public housing stock of many US cities".[11] Anyone who grew up in the 1990s and listened to hip-hop when doing so will have an idea of what Queensbridge is. It is the setting of the 1990s' darkest hip-hop records — not just "a project" but *the* projects, the ghetto. One of those places which will explain why public housing has a *bad reputation*. But

Brutalist Queensbridge Station

when you emerge from the station — another unusually spacious, Montreal-like, Brutalist cavern — you're presented with something that looks, well, pleasant. A big sign reads "WELCOME TO QUEENSBRIDGE HOUSES" in English, Spanish, Chinese and Arabic. A middle-aged man sells Penguin Classics from boxes in front of a series of low-rise Y-plan brick blocks. All around are trees, trees, trees. It does not look menacing, but as you walk deeper into it, there is something relentless about Queensbridge — a repeated rhythm starts up and just keeps going, for half a mile of brick.

Queensbridge was built at the end of the 1930s, as the third large public housing estate erected by La Guardia's New York City Housing Authority (NYCHA), and the first to be built after the 1937 Wagner-Steagall Act brought in federal funding, at the cost of much stricter rules on

Trees, Brick, Not Much Else

who could qualify for housing and how cheaply it could be built. There are lifts (the blocks go up to six storeys), but no balconies. The architecture, by one William F. Ballard, is minimal and drab: flat-fronted like the Alfred E. Smith Houses, without the big windows and smooth surfaces you might get in real Modernist housing. Its innovation, showing its adherence to Modernist planning, if not Modernist aesthetics, was *space*. The New York Ideology stresses density as a good in itself, a taste which just happens to chime with what developers would like to do anyway — packing as much lettable space as they can into the smallest possible plots. This Ideology was propagated in direct response to places like Queensbridge. Only 25% of the estate consists of building, the other 75% is green space, trees and paths. This was a model of what the New Deal city could be, a new world without landlords or slums: in 1939, when it was nearing completion, the socialists, aesthetes and hipsters compiling the *WPA Guide to New York City* listed what to expect — "twenty-six brick dwelling structures, six stories high and with elevators, a community building, and a children's centre, all arranged around open polygonal courts".[12]

You can still see all this today, and frankly, it's nice. A lot of residents are evidently elderly, and every bench on a sunny day has people sitting on it chatting to each other. A lot of older people seem to be just strolling through the tree-shaded courts, surely more pleasant than being inside in 35 degree heat (many, but not all flats have air-con units bolted to them, adding to the buildings' cheap, provisional look). You can't necessarily see it in my pictures — I thought it would have been rude to point my camera at people — but the space is *used*. There might not be "a street" here, but people are doing street things in what there is instead; and if the estate was more dense, the poverty here would be even more unadulterated, without this fresh air and light.

And Queensbridge is poor, make no mistake. Nearly 60% of tenants are on food stamps. Average family income is a staggeringly low $15,843. Without public housing and its permanently low, secure rents, fenced off from the fluctuations of the market, *none* of these people would even

Inside Queensbridge

be able to live in New York. Over the road in Long Island City, the average price of a new apartment is $1 million.[13]

Queensbridge was not *legally* segregated. In 1939, New York outlawed segregation in its public housing — nearly thirty years before the federal government did so — but it was mostly white at first. The first residents consisted of around three thousand white and fifty black families, but the improving living standards of the city's working class in the 1940s had an unexpected effect on the project. Wages were going up in the unionised, booming industries, and so many residents' income was too high to qualify for public housing under the draconian rules of the 1937 Act, which reserved it only for the poor. So in 1947, tenants who were earning good money were evicted, and low-income — mainly black and Puerto Rican — New Yorkers living in slum housing moved in. This meant that there was little continuity in tenure, no mix of classes, that the housing was conceived as a way-station, not a right — and it also meant that the city was actually *enforcing* white flight from Queensbridge. It is worth noting that the line between race and class here is very hard to draw — few places so comprehensively state Stuart Hall's claim that "race is the modality in which class is lived".[14] By the Sixties, Queensbridge was a majority-minority area, and has been so ever since. But Queensbridge didn't become notorious until the crime wave of the Seventies and the CIA-assisted crack epidemic of the Eighties, when its murder rate became one of the highest in the rich world. Something else happened in the Eighties, though — Queensbridge became the epicentre of revolution in music.

Hip-hop was invented, obviously, in the South Bronx — Queens rappers who tried to claim otherwise were put in their place in a series of furious diss tracks by Bronx denizen KRS-One — but Queensbridge was the site of two of the changes that saw it go from being a fun, novelty party music into a deeper and weirder form. In the mid-1980s, producer and Queensbridge tenant Marley Marl developed a new synthetic style of enormous kick drums and sudden stabs of noise, audibly inspired by British avant-gardists the Art of Noise (themselves inspired by the Italian Futurist manifesto for an "art of noises"), and brought in MCs who also lived in the estate, like MC Shan and Roxanne Shanté, to rap over the top, belting out ultra-confident, funny and cruel disses of named and unnamed opponents. Look up the video for Roxanne Shanté's "Roxanne's Revenge", and it looks as if they're just doing the show right there in one of their flats.[15] Marley Marl later commented, surely only half-ironically, that when these records were made, "I was paying $110 dollars a month for my rent, free electricity. So New York Housing Authority kind of co-produced some of my earlier hits. Thank you guys."[16] Roxanne Shanté lyrics are actually printed on posters here, in a series of billboards celebrating the project and its residents.

A decade later, Queensbridge was the centre of a shift towards something much more sombre, depressive, literary. Albums — not singles — like Nas' *Illmatic* or Mobb Deep's *The Infamous* were as dour as the bare brick walls of the buildings, and as complex as what went on inside, all grainy samples of mournful pianos and string arrangements over bleak, unfunky loops. Even taking into account the machismo and exaggeration of very young men (Mobb Deep, self-described "official Queensbridge murderers", were teenagers when they made their best records), the place they describe is grim; "each block is like a maze", Nas mutters in "New York State of Mind". They spoke knowingly as the feared black underclass, then being legislated against in Clinton's "one strike and you're out" laws, which mandated eviction for public housing tenants using their homes for dealing, and incarcerated hundreds of thousands of young people for petty crimes. In

"Represent", Nas is proudly "pissing in your elevator", but two tracks before in "Halftime", he tells you in passing, "I'm an intellectual". Queensbridge in these records is a dystopia of random violence; for Nas, "life is parallel to hell". Mobb Deep's third album in 1996 was just called *Hell on Earth*.

Most images of Queensbridge in hip-hop videos and record sleeves are taken from above — two long, dusty rows of red brick, at uniform height, a scar on the skyline. But on foot, it doesn't *look* like Hell on Earth. Not that I could ever know, given there is only so much you can learn from spending an hour walking around a place in daylight. But since the early 1990s crime has verifiably gone down sharply, as it has everywhere in the city. You can attribute the decline in violence in Queensbridge to whichever cause you find politically amenable. It could be owed to the authoritarian policing that has littered the place with no less than 360 CCTV cameras, and focused on frisking, following and throwing in jail scores of young black and Hispanic men, measures which, have, incidentally, at some points been supported by the local tenants' association.[17] A less bleak explanation would look at the effects of the legacy of community buildings planned and built in the late 1930s, which have been maintained and expanded over the decades by the NYCHA and local activists. These consist of a diamond-shaped high street of grocers and community centres at the crossroads of the estate, and the Jacob A. Riis Settlement, a redbrick building deep in one of the project's green courtyards.

This was one of many "settlements" sprinkled across the working-class districts of New York in the early twentieth century, on the London model of Toynbee Hall; over time, some of them have outgrown their philanthropic, *haut-en-bas* origins and become normal community centres, run by the community. This seems to have been what has happened at the Jacob A. Riis Settlement. Facing the shops and the

Socialist Realism for Seniors

junction is a simple brick building with a brightly coloured new mural; inside is a fresco dating from the building's original construction by the great painter and CPUSA fellow traveller Philip Guston. To the rear is a specialised branch of the settlement for the large population of pensioners, decorated with a more generic but still rather wonderful New Deal-era Socialist Realist low-relief sculptural panel, showing an idealised image of the Queensbridge working class indulging in the leisure pursuits made possible by their housing security. They hold aloft tennis rackets and guitars like they were hammers and sickles.

The future of a place where incomes are as low as this in the shadow of some of the most expensive property in the world is, obviously, uncertain. New York does not have an individual Right to Buy, which means places like Queensbridge have suffered far less gentrification than similar estates in London. The concomitant of Queensbridge expelling its financially comfortable residents in 1947 is that a private landlord cannot buy or let any of its flats. But recent mayors — whether the left-liberal Bill de Blasio, or neoliberals like Michael Bloomberg and the incumbent Eric Adams — have favoured staging referenda for bloc transfers of public housing to developers, who sign a guarantee to maintain rents at low levels for a set period of time.[18] This hasn't happened to Queensbridge, yet. The place has been in the news in recent years, because Amazon were planning a new HQ in Long Island City, directly opposite the estate; the president of the estate's tenants' association regularly expressed a worry they would not hire Queensbridge residents to work in their offices, and that nothing would "trickle down" to them. A local campaign against Amazon — who were due to receive $3 billion in subsidies from New York State out of gratitude for their

Long Island City, as seen from Queensbridge

moving to Queens — eventually saw the dystopian, tax-avoiding, would-be-asteroid-mining mail-order megacorp pull out.[19] The polarisation remains, even without Bezos. Serious wealth and serious poverty literally standing next to each other, separated only by a road, a Subway station and a second-hand bookstall.

Walk 4
Now We Return to Wipe out the Slum

Another candidate for the great social democratic housing complex I hadn't found in my first visit to the city had been hiding in plain sight. Walking distance from the Alfred E. Smith Houses in Two Bridges, that conglomeration of small-windowed, brick towers which I found so perturbing in 2014, is Co-Operative Village, on Grand Street in the Lower East Side. Here, over thirty years, socialists and trade unionists built an entire district of non-market, socially-owned, community-oriented Modernist housing complexes. There is *nothing* about this in some of the architecture books representing one or another facet of the New York Ideology — neither in Paul Goldberger's gushing guide to Manhattan's architecture, or in the various books I'd piled up by the sharp-witted Jane Jacobsian socialist architect and critic Michael Sorkin. I found out about it from a quite different direction — Joshua B. Freeman's 2000 history *Working-Class New York*. Although published a little too early to join the recent wave of works about post-Depression/pre-crisis reformist New York, reading this book revealed to me an entire world I had no idea existed. It is openly revisionist on this once-demonised era, making heroes of figures I had never heard of, particularly the labour leader and co-operative enthusiast Abraham Kazan. After Roosevelt Island, it was highest on my list of places I wanted to see when I came back.

Come out of East Broadway Subway Station, onto Seward Park — the first municipal park in Manhattan — and you'll immediately see the first sign that this place might be different. The Forward Building, designed in 1912, housed until 1972 the *Jewish Daily Forward*, which was for its first few decades an explicitly socialist Yiddish-language newspaper, its name taken from the German SPD's *Vorwärts*. Its architecture, designed by George Boehm, is flamboyant, in the same manner as the gilded-age Baroque office blocks of the financial district nearby: ten storeys, plaster cartouches, pediments and free-style pilasters, with the name of the paper in Yiddish at the top and in English on the brick gable-end. On the lower floors of the facade are ceramic medallions of socialist heroes — Ferdinand Lassalle, Wilhelm Liebknecht and, of course, Karl Marx and Friedrich Engels. In the 2000s, it was turned into just another block of luxury flats, but the fact those images of the founders of scientific socialism survived the McCarthy years should tell you a few things about this place. Gazing at the housing towers all around, I realised with a little disappointment that the socialist co-operatives built by these great idealists looked, from a distance, not unlike the Alfred E. Smith Houses. Windows tend to be small; there are tall, gaunt water towers on top of all of the blocks; balconies are by no means guaranteed; and everything is clad in that dark, dun brick. Understanding this was going to be complicated. Every building here has to be looked at in great detail in order to be able to differentiate it from the one next door.

The story of how Co-Operative Village came into being is an inspiring one, whatever happened next. It owes its existence to the powerful trade unions of Manhattan's once-notorious textile sweatshops. The Lower East Side was pejorative for its poor-quality tenement housing — it is one of the settings for the appalling poverty documented

Forward, Forgetting

in Jacob Riis' *How the Other Half Lives*, and explained to tourists in the district's Tenement Museum. It was also known for its atrocious working conditions, which came to more general attention with the fire at the Triangle Shirtwaist Factory of 1911, which killed 146 people, mostly women, and mostly Jewish and Italian migrants. For better or worse, the Lower East Side was famous as a centre for recently arrived immigrants, particularly Jewish escapees from what was then the Russian Empire's "Pale of Settlement", and is now eastern Poland, Ukraine, Belarus and Lithuania — the only area in which Jews were permitted to live by the brutally antisemitic Tsarist government, but where they were subject to pogroms and legally-enforced discrimination. The Lower East Side labour leaders of the period were all from the Pale, like the leader of the Amalgamated Clothing Workers, Sidney Hillman, born in 1887 in Lithuania, and David Dubinsky, born in Belarus in

1892, later the leader of the International Ladies Garment Workers Union. They were all, at first, public supporters of the Socialist Party of America. Dubinsky had been deported to Siberia for his socialist activities, but escaped to the USA; Hillman had participated in the 1905 revolution in the Tsarist Empire as a teenager. Both were moderate cadre of the Russian Social Democratic Labour Party, supporters of its Jewish Labour Bund and its Mensheviks, rather than Lenin's Bolsheviks. Among the less famous of these figures were a textile worker turned union bureaucrat at the Amalgamated, Abraham Kazan, and a young architect, Herman Jessor, both born in Ukraine in the last decades of the nineteenth century.

The Socialist Party of America — and its rogue offshoot, the Communist Party USA — had mass support round here in the first few decades of the twentieth century. It was because of this that several Socialist Party representatives were elected to the New York State Senate in Albany in 1920. They were barred from taking office on the grounds that the SPA was a seditious organisation of immigrant "aliens" devoted to the violent overthrow of the established government, which was, of course, true, up to a point. The blockage of the electoral route to even municipal socialism led to New York leftists channelling their energies into some interesting places. Abraham Kazan, as an official at the Amalgamated, suggested one winding route to socialism might be through housing. At first an anarchist, Kazan brought a distrust of the state with him into a more reformist co-operative socialism. He was a strict adherent of the "Rochdale Principles" of co-operation developed by the British labour movement — decades later, the United Housing Foundation that the textile unions created would call one of its largest projects Rochdale Village.

In the mid-1920s, Kazan took advantage of a liberalisation of housing laws and convinced the union to fund a housing co-operative in the Bronx, and another in the Lower East Side, both designed by Jessor at the firm of Springsteen and Goldhammer. The Lower East Side co-operative, Amalgamated Dwellings, completed in 1930, is the earliest part of Co-Operative Village, and a short walk from the Forward Building. Jessor's design is instantly recognisable to the socialist architecture aficionado as being inspired by the superblocks of "Red Vienna", the socialist state-within-a-state that thrived in the 1920s. The buildings are arranged around a semi-public courtyard, symmetrical, proud and ever so slightly grandiose. The textured bright red brickwork was both a use of a local material — used in the mammoth nearby Knickerbocker Village, a contemporary private endeavour to build profitable "affordable housing" in one enormous cliff of interminable flats — and maybe a little comment on the politics of the project.[1] In 1939, the authors of the *WPA Guide to New York* paused to approve the Amalgamated Dwellings as an alternative to charity and philanthropy: "the architecture diverts the eye with parabolic archways, and a surface patterning of brick designs and stucco inserts", which gives the complex "a certain charm and human quality" lacking from the likes of Knickerbocker Village.[2] There are allotments as part of the estate, a touch which immediately evokes the world of labour to anyone from the UK; but Amalgamated Dwellings looked a little tired in 2022, obviously midway through some interminable renovation, with the courtyard scaffolded and fenced off. A Georgian "settlement house" can be found next door; along with a redbrick church and the tiny stone Bialystoker Synagogue, a conversion of a very south Wales stone Methodist chapel from the 1820s, it is one of a handful of survivors from the enormous slum clearance that happened to the area after the Second World War.

Red Vienna, Red Manhattan

The socialists of the Lower East Side had a role in the construction of an American welfare state of sorts in the Roosevelt years and onwards, but it was necessarily a subsidiary one. Most socialists in New York supported the New Deal, and hence the Democrat Franklin Delano Roosevelt for president and the Republican Fiorello La Guardia for mayor (La Guardia had even once stood for election as a Socialist Party candidate); but they tried, like the DSA today, to keep one foot in and one foot out of the USA's two-capitalist-parties system. In the Thirties, New York labour organisers like Hillman and Dubinsky, who were suspicious of a leftwards turn in the Socialist Party and hostile to the Communist Party, formed a new American Labor Party. Its purpose was largely to support Roosevelt and La Guardia without joining either the party of Southern segregationists or the party of Northern big business. When the Labor Party and Hillman then moved closer to the CPUSA, a faction under Dubinsky set up a rival American Liberal Party, again with the purpose of supporting labour-sympathetic bourgeois politicians.[3] So the New York socialists were bridesmaids rather than brides in the never universal, always partial welfare state that FDR and his successors built in the Thirties. But in and around Grand Street, you could think as you walked around that they'd actually managed to run the place.

For Joshua Freeman, the massive expansion of public welfare in New York was unique in the country, and owed to the peculiar strength and ambition of its labour movement. Nowhere in the USA would ever have a universal welfare state of the kind normal in Europe, East Asia, Australasia and Canada, with decommodified healthcare and guaranteed, country-wide social benefits.[4] In the industrial Midwest, the unions — which had their own insurgent moment in the massive Congress of Industrial Organisations (CIO) strikes in Detroit, Chicago, Pittsburgh, et al in the Thirties — used their vast but localised strength to build a kind of private welfare state, where the company would insure workers' healthcare, pensions and sick pay. In the south and west, there was practically no welfare state at all, bar the bare-bones system Roosevelt set up. As a result of this, as the socialist journalist and future DSA leader Michael Harrington wrote in 1962, in the US "the welfare state benefits least those who need help most".[5] New York came closest to catering for those people as well. It created a vast system which encompassed housing, health care, schools, colleges, transport. Unlike in the Midwest, it covered many more people than just unionised company workers, and it encouraged public transport and urban housing, rather than cars and suburbia; but it was also never quite a universal welfare state on the social democratic model.

Instead, Freeman writes, "a hybrid form of municipal social democracy" which "included state action, an ever-increasing range of services provided directly by unions, and huge labor-linked cooperatives and service organisations"[6] came into being between the Thirties and Seventies. It was reinforced in harsh regulations on private landlordism: "in 1950 the New York state government regulated 96 percent of the rental units and nearly 80 percent of housing of any kind in New York City".[7] The city maintained wartime rent controls, while the rest of the USA, including New York state, abandoned them. The pound of flesh for all of this was collaboration with Washington in the Cold War. Many — if not all — of these socialist labour leaders were already anti-communists, and needed no convincing to oppose the Soviets abroad, but as America's imperial wars became ever more bloodthirsty and indefensible — culminating in the apocalypse rained down on Vietnam by Kennedy and Johnson — these old leftists found themselves the enemies of an anti-imperialist New Left. For the young Maoist printworker who led a rent strike in one of Kazan's housing projects, Kazan and his Lower East Side housing activists were simply "social democratic whores".[8]

For Kazan and Hillman, co-operatives — rather than public housing — were the best means to creating an

American welfare state, quite possibly because they offered a distance from a state in Washington which would likely always be hostile to any kind of socialism. Yet smarter capitalists were also supportive of co-ops, among them the unlikely friend of the workers John D. Rockefeller Jr, who had ordered the killing of scores of striking miners in the Colorado Coalfield War of the 1910s. As one recent history of New York's workers' co-ops writes, though a "staunch conservative", Rockefeller "favoured cooperative housing as a way to head off public housing",[9] and funded several co-ops in the 1920s. Rockefeller realised that co-ops were, essentially, a form of owner-occupation, and hence potentially useful in the much more important project of heading off and discrediting any genuine decommodification of American housing. Over the decades, as the co-operative movement grew, more complex and very much capitalist finance became necessary to build ever larger housing projects. Moreover, it cemented a two — or in NYC, three-or-four-tier — housing system, with public housing at the bottom.

Back on Grand Street, you can see the results of the post-war co-op expansion on either side of Amalgamated Dwellings. The earliest additions were the Hillman Co-Operative Houses, built in 1950 and named after the labour leader who had sponsored them before his death; one of the blocks is named after Meyer London, a Socialist Party of America member several times elected to Washington as a Congressman for the Lower East Side. They are in red brick, like the Amalgamated blocks, but by comparison a little sprawling and slightly ungainly, with zig-zag layouts, as at Queensbridge designed to keep plenty of sun and air circulating around the flats. Decoration has been limited to some fluting and carving of the brick around the lower floors. But the green public spaces are in much better condition, lush, generous and offering much needed breeze and shelter in the July heat. The success of these blocks attracted the attention of New York's head of slum clearance, who was, naturally, the always multitasking Robert Moses. Moses helped Kazan and the Amalgamated to set up the United Housing Foundation (UHF), with backing from the city, New York state and an alliance of trade unions. The UHF would be prime movers as Moses proceeded to order the demolition of around half of the Lower East Side. Moses, who had no time for socialists, nonetheless admired Kazan and Jessor as people who *got things done*. The new UHF's logo, depicting twin pine trees, spoke of nobler goals: it symbolised the two aims of the organisation. "To serve. Not to profit." These pines stand inset into brick gates on either side of the entrance to Hillman Houses, along with a quote from the great man about the future of America, etched into stone. "We want a better America... where no child will cry out for food in the midst of plenty. An America that will have no sense of insecurity and which will make it possible for all groups regardless of race colour or creed to live in friendship, to be real neighbors."

Again, the system used to try to build this was complicated. The funding of the next phases of Co-Operative Village made use of the post-war housing acts, and of the 1955 Mitchell-Lama Act passed in New York state, which mandated public funding for "middle-income" housing intended to fill the gap between public housing for the poor and market housing for the affluent. Mitchell-Lama offered tax breaks for developers who would agree to a cap on the amount of rent or mortgage they could legally charge, set at below 30% of the average wage. The UHF availed itself of Mitchell-Lama funding, but specifically favoured the "limited-equity" co-operative model. This meant in practice that residents owned equal shares in the co-op and paid a carrying charge, but did not own their

Entrance to Hillman Houses

property outright; they could sell the shares, not their flats. The price of a deposit was capped; as in Swedish co-ops of the time, your flat reverts to the co-op when you die. But the Mitchell-Lama programme, which funded the co-ops along with dozens of other new housing developments across NYC, mandated that after twenty years there was an option to revert to the private market, placing a bomb under the whole thing. It all sounds needlessly complex, but these were the instruments the UHF used to set up two huge new co-ops along Grand Street.

East River Housing Co-Operative, opened in 1956, was the first of these; its principal sponsor was the International Ladies Garment Workers Union. David Dubinsky, as leader of the ILGWU, gave a speech when the foundations were laid in 1953, in which he linked the buildings to the long-running project to bury the squalid, ruthlessly exploitative world he had escaped to from a Siberian prison camp four decades earlier. In the Lower East Side, the labour movement's first aim had been to fight a "war against the sweatshop"; having won that by the 1950s, the UHF showed the working class would "return to wipe out the slum".[10] This concentration on memory could also be seen in the names given to the blocks. One was jointly named after Henryk Ehrlich and Wiktor Alter, the Polish leaders of the Jewish Labour Bund who were murdered on Stalin's orders in 1942; a block each was named after labour leaders Benjamin Schlesinger and Morris Sigman; and another took the name of Morris Hillquit, a leader of the Socialist Party of America who in 1917 fought an impressive campaign for Mayor of New York, winning over 20% of the vote. These are all reminders of what was important to this generation of moderate socialists — commemorating anti-Stalinist socialists and remembering the crimes of the Soviet Union, commemorating the workplace struggles of the recent past, and recalling the labour movement's role in ending housing squalor.

The East River Co-Operative, and the subsequent Seward Park Housing Co-Operative (1961), is built to a standard type, a cross-planned slab, with good, wide balconies, and recessed upper floors, in the setback style of a New York skyscraper, all in green space. It's a good standard, and the UHF used it again in their next development further uptown, Penn South, which I had glimpsed in 2014 from the High Line. It's not craft building anymore, but an elegant and necessarily repetitious module. With these three estates, the UHF got into standardisation in a big way, with the resulting savings being ploughed into exacting interior specifications. Each flat is dual aspect, with cross-ventilation, large combined kitchen-dining-rooms and central air-conditioning. Joshua Freeman notes that the standards extended to parquet floors, and an accompanying

The Co-Operative Village in the City

programme of co-operative shops, community centres, sports facilities, corner shops and clubs.[11]

As the architect and hence the public face, Jessor got much of the criticism for the standard designs, and insisted the amenities could only be paid for by restricting anything fancy on the facades. But there is still a certain drama to these buildings; after walking around them for a while, you'll find that East River and Seward Park's stepped towers do have a definite pride and vigour in their scale. Seward Park even has a rare touch of artistic relief in the lobbies of its four great slab blocks, with glorious New Deal murals of Albert Einstein, Thomas Jefferson, Abraham Lincoln and Franklin D. Roosevelt, painted by the Communist artist Hugo Gellert. But these remain enormous buildings, in relentless brick — when the repetitiousness of his designs were criticised in the press during the Sixties,

Jessor quipped "the cheapest wall is still a brick wall".[12] It is all a little sad — the architects of social housing at the same time in much of the wealthy world did not have to make these calculations, and created buildings that are beautiful rather than merely functional. Why the richest and most powerful city in the richest and most powerful country in the world built its social housing more like that of, say, Poland or East Germany than like that of Sweden, Austria or Britain is enduringly mysterious. The New Deal corporatist gloss of a Rockefeller Center, with all its marble and gold and chrome, feels a very long way away.

In any case, by the time of Seward Park, Jane Jacobs was paying attention, and counted Kazan and Jessor as destroyers of the "ballet of the street", and inveterate creators of "radiant garden city beautiful". Certainly, Kazan, who had spent more than enough of his life in the Lower East Side slums, cared nothing for historic architecture —

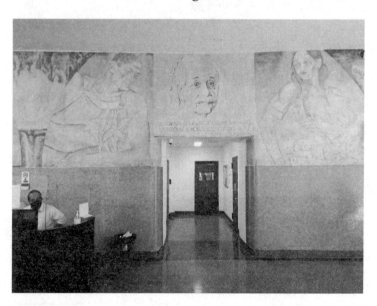

Einstein's Lobby

"history has always been made by people, not buildings".[13] Kazan also pointed out that Jacobs' notion that slum clearance would lead to a loosening of social bonds simply wasn't borne out in the well-used communal facilities of UHF projects.[14] Jessor was similarly unapologetic. The "social fabric" that "Jane Jacobs and her ilk" purported to find in the slums, he argued, "does not exist. The people living in the miserable slums are not there by choice". But everybody in the UHF projects *was*. He put it with considerable frankness — "the only solution is large-scale urban renewal — the 'Bulldozer approach'".[15] Clear out all the buildings, and their landlords with them, and start again. The victims in this Faustian pact were those residents in the slum clearances Moses forced through and Kazan assisted, afflicting especially those who could not afford to put down a deposit on a co-operative flat. The areas of the Lower East Side the UHF were building in were, by the Fifties, in very large part Puerto Rican and black as well as Jewish; but the co-ops were overwhelmingly Jewish. Residents opposed the slum clearances, not out of attachment to their dilapidated, slumlord-dominated homes, but for the obvious reason that most of them would not have been able to afford to live in the co-ops. Some of those cleared did move into Seward Park Co-Operative, but more went into public housing.[16]

The UHF were not satisfied by the enormous slashes they'd made into the slums — in the early Sixties, they made plans to raze what was left of the old Lower East Side, replacing it with more towers-in-a-park by Jessor. They abandoned this when City Hall demanded a greater variety of building types, as a reaction to criticism of East River and Seward Park's standardised designs. The UHF wouldn't build anything but slabs out of principle — their own calculations showed that architectural variety would have meant co-operators' carrying charges going up by around a quarter. Kazan asserted that "we do not now accept the theory that the exterior design of a building is worth the difference of $7.00 a room per month to the man of low and moderate income", simply in order "to make the city supposedly more attractive architecturally".[17] So after this, the UHF developed only in non-slum clearance sites, like the UDC did in developments like Roosevelt Island. The last UHF estates were enormous, with their own co-operative supermarkets and power stations. Rochdale Village in Queens housed 25,000 people, Co-Op City in the Bronx a staggering 44,000, and Twin Pines in Brooklyn, 14,000. The latter was privatised mid-construction and renamed Starrett City when the UHF collapsed as a result of the 1970s fiscal crisis. The proximate cause for the UHF's downfall was a carrying-charge strike by the residents of Co-Op City, as the Old and New lefts fought bitterly in what proved to be a case of mutually-assured destruction. The banks took over the wreckage.[18]

The housing remains. And it's good — and so are the public spaces. Critics of the "project" model, of towers-in-a-park and other contraventions of the New York Ideology, cannot begin to explain how pleasant it is to weave your way through these green spaces, with the steel girders of Williamsburg Bridge and the flickering light of the East River emerging at unexpected moments out of all the brick — utterly urban, and enlivened by birdsong. The rows of shops and community centres built to supplement the abstract slabs in space obviously work well in the 2020s: none are derelict, all are lively, and the place has also, with its active kosher markets and synagogues, clearly remained a substantially Jewish area, with residents refusing the opportunity to move to the suburbs or Florida. It all seems to work just fine. I did not visit the larger UHF projects like Rochdale Village or Co-Op City so I can't comment on their qualities, but the original Jacobsian objection to such spaces makes most sense as a fear of what would happen to an area's community ties and its general legibility if it was *just* towers in a park. But these towers are always close to high streets and public spaces, and are very much in the heart of things. Their combined density and spaciousness allows a resident to have their cake and eat it — enjoy peace, quiet and greenery, *and* the bustle and noise and activity of a real city. In rejecting this, we have lost a great deal.

The more convincing criticism of the UHF co-ops is their relation to public housing, and the hierarchical system of non-market housing the project implied. There is a lot of public housing in the Lower East Side — one reason why all those streets are so enjoyable to walk in, and have so few branches of Starbucks or estate agents — and at first, you will struggle to work out what is the product of the UHF and what is the product of the NYCHA. In theory, it should be easy to tell what is public and what is private — so much

Ballet of the Non-Street

of the case against public housing rests on this, on the "stigma" against non-market housing, instantly identifiable from the outside. But I had to go through gazetteers and online forums for weeks until I could work out what was what in the Lower East Side. I had assumed the repetitive point blocks you can see just behind the East River complex, framing a rustic red brick Romanesque church, were part of the UHF development. They are actually Grand Street Guild Houses, a public housing complex built not by the NYCHA, but sponsored by the Catholic Church and funded by the federal department of Housing and Urban Development (HUD). It was completed in 1973 but looks much earlier, and shows the benefit of a recent renovation, looking clean and crisp.

Looking far worse are the La Guardia Houses, a NYCHA estate of cross-plan point blocks built between 1959 and 1965. These have balconies, but are marred by the ugly

Catholic Social

patching up of damaged brickwork, which makes the towers look cheap and squalid. Herman Jessor might have been right that a brick wall was the cheapest and simplest wall to build, but La Guardia Houses shows it was possible for budgets to be set low enough to screw up even this. Opposite these are the complex slabs of Baruch Houses, designed by Emory Roth for NYCHA, and opened in 1959. These are in better condition, and resemble Queensbridge in their zig-zag layout and their brown brickwork; their green spaces are currently under the threat of an 'infill' plan to fix the NYCHA's parlous finances by building market housing in the interstices of its housing projects.

At either end of the area are two projects, each in the mandatory dark reddish-brown brick, which show just how attractive and unattractive public housing could be here. Right by East Broadway station is NYCHA's Seward Park Extension, a 1973 design by William Pedersen, founder of the

Brick Patchup at La Guardia Houses

giant corporate firm Kohn Pedersen Fox. It consists of a tower
and a quite formal walled courtyard with a playground inside;
it's impressive as pure architecture, with its articulated brick
façade twisted into a complicated pattern to accommodate
balconies and setbacks, with its obligatory water tower
appearing as a neat corner turret rather than the usual
accidental excrescence. It suggests that City Hall, then under
the Republican but Liberal Party-affiliated John Lindsay
administration, knew what they were doing in rejecting the
UHF's designs for the same site. But walk round the corner,
and you're at the NYCHA's Rutgers Houses, from only a
decade earlier — a series of genuinely shockingly bleak tiny-
windowed, flat-fronted slabs, without relief or visual interest
(or balconies), examples of pure human-warehousing. And
yet: it does what it is meant to do. Just behind the blocks
is a pleasant, leafy little park. As the authors of *Affordable
Housing in New York* point out, the many Projects in the Lower
East Side are today "an island of permanent, below-market
rents in an area that has rapidly gentrified", and without
them, "virtually all of these families would have had to leave
the neighbourhood".[19] You can see what is coming next
everywhere. Between Rutgers Houses and Manhattan Bridge
is something called One Manhattan Square, a 72-storey
private glass tower that shuns the neighbourhood, hard up
against the river. It was allowed to be built on the proviso
that "affordable housing" would be built by the developer
alongside; so a much smaller, cheaper-looking block stands
alongside, a little bit of "trickle-down" in action.[20]

This sort of social neoliberalism — let developers do
what they like here, and we'll eke out a little bit of affordable
housing there — is shamed by the sheer extent of what the
city council, the trade unions and the churches built here
between the Thirties and Seventies. But that experiment
had its own limits, paradoxically created specifically *by* the
communalist "diversity" of New York's social movements.

Public Housing as Sculpture

Rutgers Houses and One Manhattan Square

What looks like a diverse area in the park and in the Subway station (and, I expect, the schools) is actually parcelled into several distinct redbrick silos for different ethnic groups. The public housing estates are mainly black, Puerto Rican and sometimes Chinese; the UHF co-operatives are mainly Jewish; the renovated socialist newspaper offices and new luxury enclaves built in the interstices may be diverse in everything other than class.

The co-ops round here have not all availed themselves of the opportunity to sell up; the residents of the pale brick slabs of Masaryk Towers, for instance, a cookie-cutter Mitchell-Lama estate nearby, voted recently *against* privatisation. Co-Operative Village, however, voted to privatise in 1997. In a sense this is unsurprising, as doing so is a licence to print money (flats there now go for around $1 million, to a different class of co-operator), but it set them apart from the residents of the UHF's Penn South estate a couple of miles away, who overwhelmingly voted to stay affordable around the same time.[21] One recent study argues that the rationale for this was largely racial: the fear that when elderly co-operators died and their flats were open to the waiting list, new black and Puerto Rican co-operators would move in. This is indeed what happened in the now majority-black UHF estates of Co-Op City and Rochdale Village, though the class make-up of these has stayed resolutely the same as intended — skilled labourers, transport workers, postal workers, lower-paid office clerks, municipal employees, still exactly earning the New York average wage. But at Co-Operative Village, this gradual transition was resisted. In the late Seventies, black and Puerto Rican New Yorkers whose applications to live in Co-Operative Village were ignored or declined without good reason sued the management, which lost the case. It was given racial quotas by the courts to redress the balance; privatisation was one way to control the waiting list that the courts couldn't influence. The move was certainly not unopposed; residents remembered "screaming matches in the laundries", and co-operators proclaiming that if the sell-off went through, Abraham Kazan would turn in his grave.[22] As it is, the truly enduringly affordable homes here are now in the mixed bunch of public housing slabs and towers around.

Past the crossroads of "Dimes Square", a tiny gentrified junction known for its edgelord art scene, and you're in Chinatown; the Hebrew-script signs with smaller text below in English abruptly give way to Chinese-character signs with smaller text below in English. The old tenements still stand, and if you're looking online for a cheap place to stay in Manhattan, it's here or nowhere — booking websites abound with fairly affordable if perhaps insalubrious short-stays here. Chinatown too has its own example of heroic communitarian Modernism, in the shape of Confucius Plaza, an enormous redbrick tower built as a predominantly Chinese affordable Mitchell-Lama co-operative; flat-fronted on one side, it then curves round to create something more sculptural than Herman Jessor managed with that straitened palette of brick and glass. Its construction inadvertently elicited one of the pivotal struggles of the new, anti-imperialist and anti-racist left. While it was going up in 1975, the contractors refused to use Chinese building workers, claiming, obviously outrageously, that they were too physically weak. A protest was organised by a group called Asian Americans for Equal Employment (AAEE), who kicked up enough of a stink that in the end several Chinese-American labourers were hired to help construct the block. Here, history then repeated itself.

One of the rediscovered cult books of the American New Left circa 2023 is Max Elbaum's *Revolution in the Air*, all but ignored on publication in 2002 but recently republished with a glowing introduction by one of the lead organisers of Black Lives Matter, Alicia Garza, suggesting these are the acknowledged precursors of this amorphous but huge movement which in 2020 led possibly the biggest protests in US history. *Revolution in the Air* took as its subject the

New Communist Movement — the umbrella term for the proliferation of sometimes comradely, sometimes warring Marxist-Leninist sects that emerged in the wake of the Black Panthers and the American 1968, who liked to refer to the country as "Amerika" for some reason. For those who *don't* believe in repeating the experiment of socialists attempting to radicalise the Democratic Party — the assumption that such a thing is possible is fundamental to the strategies of the DSA and Bernie Sanders — Elbaum's book has become a touchstone.[23] One of the Guevarist and Maoist sects Elbaum describes, the Workers Viewpoint Organisation, created AAEE and organised the protests at Confucius Plaza.[24] In the aftermath of this successful struggle, the group was reformed as Asian Americans for Equality (AAFE), which, in strikingly similar manner to the socialists of the Twenties and Thirties, moved quickly into housing reform — mainly through taking over and renovating as affordable housing the old "slum" properties the UHF didn't manage to demolish, though they built some small new infill buildings as well. AAFE have built no large-scale "projects", but then, the Nixon administration's official (and still unended) moratorium on funding any more public and state-subsidised housing, passed in 1973, means it is doubtful they could have even if they wanted to.

With the UHF long gone, AAFE are today the largest actually existing developers of affordable housing in Lower Manhattan;[25] like the UHF they have apparently moved gradually towards the city's housing establishment and away from their Marxist roots. They were not the only Maoists in Chinatown: one of the largest New Communist organisations was I Wor Kuen ("Righteous and Harmonious Fists"), which aimed at becoming something like a Chinese Black Panther Party. In the late 1970s, I Wor Kuen dissolved itself into a unity organisation, the League of Revolutionary Struggle, which had the poet and critic Amiri Baraka among its leaders. By the mid-1980s it was helping to organise Jesse Jackson's Presidential bid, the Sanders campaign of its day. The same questions return here, again and again — to resist and defend, or to construct something new? To try to influence a corrupt, closed, two-party system, or shun it? A hundred years now of this deadlock — will the young socialists be able to break out of it? For all their numbers, they haven't even begun to build.

Walk 5
Leftovers from the Meat-Axe

In the eight days I spent in New York City in July 2022, I was staying at a hotel in the South Bronx. That is, in the area which more than any other is at the heart of the New York Ideology's creation/destruction myth. During the Seventies and Eighties, the South Bronx saw perhaps the greatest devastation ever inflicted on a rich city in peacetime. Depopulated by most of its white residents, pockmarked with much more public housing than Manhattan, with a gigantic expressway ploughed through it, the South Bronx was subject to a series of arson attacks by its slumlords, knowing that they could make more money out of insurance than from lettings. As a result, entire blocks of the area were ruined, derelict or empty by 1980. It is the blasted landscape you can see in all of those films of the late 1970s and early 1980s, looking something like Warsaw in 1944. It was also, at exactly this time, the birthplace of hip-hop, created by the block parties thrown by the Jamaican immigrant DJ Kool Herc, in the community centre of 1520 Sedgwick Avenue, a Mitchell-Lama tower in Morris Heights.[1]

The decision to stay here was not, I promise, motivated by wanting to *rough it*, so much as by requiring somewhere I could afford which was actually in one of the five boroughs. The hotel in question had been blamed for the NYC Legionnaire's Disease outbreak a few years ago, but I felt that if anywhere was likely no longer to give you

Legionnaire's Disease, it was the hotel publicly blamed for the outbreak. The Opera House Hotel is in the Beaux-Arts-style Bronx Opera House, which takes up a stretch of the Hub, a busy junction of shops, offices and tenements between the districts of Mott Haven and Melrose. There is nothing of the original architecture inside, but posters and framed photographs document a bygone world of the Marx Brothers, Mae West and bobbed dancing girls. Most of the people staying there, insofar as I could ascertain from looking around me at breakfast, were either white out-of-towners of modest means or South Asian families visiting relatives. The rooms are big, air-conditioned against the wall of heat outside and have baths. The Subway takes you to Midtown Manhattan in fifteen minutes. I had nothing to complain about.

New Yorkers, like Londoners, like to talk about the complete and total gentrification of their city. While this draws on a real and true problem — the unaffordability, unless you've got a council (or NYCHA or Mitchell-Lama or rent-controlled) flat, of previously low-rent areas like Dalston, Peckham, Greenwich Village or the Lower East Side — let's admit it can tend towards an exaggeration of trends. There are no Cereal Cafés or places that serve skin-contact wine or whatever the current irritant is in Edmonton, Southall, Mitcham or Thamesmead, and there are none in the Hub, either. It is obviously overwhelmingly working class, and though incredibly diverse, has a very small white population — around 2%, which would be highly unusual even in a diverse area of London; it is the obvious flipside of the equally noticeable whiteness of the Midtown and Downtown neighbourhoods I had walked around in 2014. I had of course been warned, I think at least in part as a joke, about gentrification in the South Bronx. And yes, there is construction along the river in Mott Haven, with luxury glass towers on former industrial sites, exploiting the proximity of Uptown Manhattan — "The Bronx is Back, Baby!" crowed one recent headline in the *Wall Street Journal*. But you wouldn't necessarily know it in the Hub. While the Lower East Side resembles a London area like Peckham or Hackney in the way new upper-middle-class housing and lower-middle- and working-class social housing rub close up against each other, here the posh flats feel a distance away, like one of those London riverside spots like Deptford or Rotherhithe where the glass and trespa riverside stands in front of and disconnected from a hinterland of Modernist estates and Victorian detritus.

The weird and arbitrary nature of racial classifications is obvious enough here, in much the same way as "white" in the mid-century US encompassed Italians, Jews, Poles and Irish, along with the local WASP upper class, as one apparently coherent bloc. In the most recent breakdown I could find, 33% of the South Bronx's residents are "black",

South Bronx, South South Bronx

but that includes African-Americans, Afro-Caribbeans and Sub-Saharan Africans (sixteen African languages are spoken round here). The 61% that is "Hispanic" might include Puerto Ricans whose families have been here since the Thirties, recent Guatemalan or Ecuadorian migrants, or any number of other backgrounds. What most of them have in common is poverty. 37% of people in Mott Haven are listed as living in poverty, with an income of $22,000 for a family of three; it is the second poorest place in New York, after nearby Morrisania, also in the South Bronx, where 40% are in poverty.[2] You can see it on the streets, in the same way as in any devastated post-industrial area anywhere. The amount of people on crutches or in wheelchairs is alarming; a certain amount of people are visibly not OK. But then, most people look like they're just on their way to work. The big store on the corner by the hotel sells with its cheap underwear and T-shirts various kinds of scrubs, for employees of the Lincoln Hospital five minutes' walk away.

Architecturally, the area resembles a piece of Manhattan that has been battered and shrunk. The Hub is fancifully called the South Bronx's Broadway, its Times Square, but there's no neon or glitz to be seen (though mercifully, there is also no branch of Planet Hollywood). There are some fun buildings, worth lingering over — the miniature three-storey redbrick bonsai Flatiron Building squeezed into the sharp point of the intersection; the attractive Hanseatic Gothic redbrick church; the Beaux-Arts mini-skyscraper of 369 East 149th Street; and there is block after block after redbrick block of iron-escaped tenements, each of which has somehow survived the ravages of the Seventies. They would no doubt be very expensive and chic in Manhattan, but here, they're slum housing still, and one explanation for the NYCHA's enormous waiting list. In the near distance are sheer brown brick slabs of the area's public housing, like

NYCHA's Melrose Houses

Melrose Houses, erected in 1952; appropriately, there's a Hip-Hop Museum nearby.

There is even a little new construction. All those new towers for Manhattanites on the river have trickled down a little to the Hub in the form of La Central, a 100% affordable housing and YMCA complex opposite the Opera House. It is, just like the housing of the Fifties-to-the-Seventies, in a dour redbrick grid, with prefabricated brick panels now rather than entire walls. The design, by FX Collaborative and MHG Architects, is a little dour, but intelligent enough within its budget in the way it negotiates the sharp corners of the Hub's junctions and in the public spaces nestled between and on top of the blocks.[3] Next to it is a glass office block apparently soon to become a Charter School, the private, for-profit, union-opposed genre of school similar to the UK's "City Academies". As trickledown goes, I have

Actually Existing New Social Housing

seen worse, here and in London, but it is telling that the "affordable" crumbs are being put here, not in Manhattan.

There is activity everywhere — images of the area circa 1980 are deceptive. One thing the Hub is *not* is desolate, and unlike in Queensbridge, there was no way I could direct my camera away from people; I only realised days later that a picture I had taken of Melrose Houses had a man picking a bin in the foreground. There are people hanging out on every corner, sat out, sometimes on fold-up chairs, enjoying the weather, and it's mostly good to see, though a lot of people tend to talk to each other in a tone that suggests they think they're on TV. A year before, weed-smoking was legalised by New York state, and you could smell it everywhere, though the results appeared to be on the mellow more than the paranoid side. I found anyone I actually spoke to was friendly, and sometimes kind beyond the call of politeness, as when everyone on the street huddled beneath the awning of the scrubs purveyor during a sudden rainstorm. The Subway, which I took several times a day, was something else. On the hottest day, at 37 degrees, a man sold cold water while sitting on the steps, calling out "Cold water, $1 dollar"; as I passed, he called out "Uptown guy, cold water, $1 dollar", the only time in those eight days that my being a white English person wandering round in a shirt and linen trousers was noted to my face. The Subway was brutally hot (and made more so by the air-conditioning of the trains), so stifling that I constantly would wander up and down the platform until the train arrived to keep cool. You enter the Subway through narrow turnstiles, one set to get in, one to get out, and a large gate between can be pushed open in emergencies, setting off an alarm. I do not exaggerate in stating that this alarm was on, constantly. One morning a man in a wheelchair, unconscious, was slumped at the end of the platform, having soiled himself. The ubiquitous NYPD officers seemed not to have noticed.

No doubt he, whatever happened to him, was here because of the proximity of Lincoln Hospital. This long-standing hospital complex is one of the surviving fragments of New York's social democratic state-within-a-state, one of eleven publicly owned hospitals treating millions of New Yorkers, including the half a million of them without private health insurance. Architecturally, the current building is typical Seventies reformed Brutalism, in a hard, bright redbrick, its sides sculpted into fortress turrets, overlooking a railway line and a bridge; the designers were Urbahn Associates, later responsible for the horrible Tombs in Manhattan. It has its own small role in New York's Marxist-Leninist history — in 1970, the hospital was occupied by members of the local chapter of the Young

Lords Party, which had begun as a Puerto Rican street gang, attained class consciousness, and reconstructed itself into an anti-imperialist class struggle organisation.[4] Pointing to systematic discrimination in the hospital against the needs of the increasingly predominant black and Hispanic population, the occupiers actually saw their demands accepted by the hospital management; they were allowed to run community health programmes for the hospital in the aftermath. The dominance of the hospital over the area is very noticeable; one of many former industrial areas where tending to the diseases of capitalism (rates of asthma and diabetes are sky-high here) has replaced factory production.[5]

Opposite are flats — Michaelangelo Apartments, designed by Weiner & Gran. It is a rectilinear, city-block-sized Mitchell-Lama complex of 1974 with shops, a market and cafés on the ground floor and towers

The Paranoid Style in American Hospital Architecture

above, all in a grid of concrete and pale orange brick. It is another product, like Roosevelt Island, of the UDC under Ed Logue, and showcases more quietly that body's attempt to reform the planning, and not the aesthetics, of project Modernism. There are no concessions to historical precedent or indeed, to visual pleasure of any kind on the elevations, but the planning is interesting in trying to square the same circle as Roosevelt Island. The street-focused integration of shops and flats clearly works well, looking as if a standard NYCHA/Mitchell-Lama product was adapted in line with the arguments of Jane Jacobs. From here, cross the railway bridge and you're on the mythic Grand Concourse.

In truth, outside New York, the Grand Concourse — the street and its surrounding area — is mythic only to those of us who read at an impressionably young age Marshall Berman's *All That Is Solid Melts Into Air*. In that dialectical

Towers on a Street

tightrope-walk between a Modernism from below and a Modernism from above, the Grand Concourse, a boulevard developed in the interwar years in the southwest Bronx, then a mainly Jewish and passionately left-wing area, features prominently. The eulogy to the Concourse comes after a description of the horrors wreaked by planning blight, landlordism and the enormous slices cut out of the city by Robert Moses in creating decades of public housing complexes and then blasting the Cross-Bronx Expressway through what remained:

> I can remember standing above the construction site for the Cross-Bronx Expressway, weeping for my neighbourhood... vowing remembrance and revenge... The Grand Concourse, from whose heights I watched and thought, was our borough's closest thing to a Parisian boulevard. Among its most striking features were rows of large, splendid 1930s apartment houses: simple and clear in their architectural forms, whether geometrically sharp or biomorphically curved; brightly coloured in contrasting brick, offset with chrome, beautifully interplayed with large areas of glass.

He continues: "the style of these buildings, known as Art Deco today, was called 'modern' in their prime. For my parents, who described our family proudly as a 'modern' family, the Concourse buildings represented a pinnacle of modernity. We couldn't afford to live in them", Berman notes, but, he insists, "they could still be admired for free, like the rows of glamorous ocean liners in port downtown". But the tragedy was that "here in the Bronx, the modernity of the urban boulevard was being condemned as obsolete, and blown to pieces, by the modernity of the interstate highway".[6]

The emptiness of the South Bronx was a terrible fulfilment of a process of de-densification and emptying-out that Moses had begun with the aim of wiping out the slums. In 1949, Moses predicted that fifty years hence, "a fourth of The Bronx will remain field, forest, and stream".[7] As the epigraph for his chapter on the South Bronx, Berman quotes and slightly abridges a notorious Moses line, which he stated when subjected to criticism for demolishing such huge swathes of the city. The full quote is as follows:

> You can draw any kind of picture you like on a clean slate and indulge your every whim in the wilderness in laying out a New Delhi, Canberra or Brasília, but when you operate in an overbuilt metropolis, you have to hack your way with a meat ax.[8]

The South Bronx today is what survived the butcher; it might not have survived at all. By 1976, Mayor Abraham Beame's chief housing officer, Roger Starr — who had undergone an ever-rightwards transition, not uncommon among his generation of intellectuals, from Trotskyism to social democracy to neoconservatism — declared that the future of the Bronx was "planned shrinkage". That is, the deliberate divestment and abandonment by the government and business of the South Bronx, both to a much smaller population, and to nature. Close not just the factories, but the hospitals, the schools, the Subway stations. Obsessed with crime and with the allegedly workshy "culture" of Puerto Ricans and blacks, Starr lamented that social democratic housing policy had been based on taking "the peasant" from the plantations of the South or the Caribbean and trying to make an urban worker out of him. "Why not keep him a peasant?"[9]

I wanted to see what was left of this place, and see what of Berman's "Modernism in the streets" had survived the assault. "Moses", Berman wrote with acuity, "was destroying our world, yet he seemed to be working in the name of values that we ourselves embraced". Jewish socialists like Berman's parents believed in public hospitals and public housing and housing co-operatives, and believed in the state doing things for people, only to have that faith repaid in the concerted destruction of everything they had made their own. By the 1970s, the area round the Concourse had experienced major white flight, whether to the then still very white suburbs of New Jersey, Westchester County and beyond, or to the UHF's Co-Op City, which was much more racially mixed but similarly based on establishing a distance from what the Concourse had become — traffic-choked, dilapidated, violent and no longer populated by *people like us*. But interestingly, very little of the Concourse itself was destroyed by the landlords' arson offensive. It was declared a Historic District a decade or so ago, with a dedicated website telling you who designed each building, how old it is and what it is made of, with a wave of listings making sure they can't be pulled down.

But a walk there from the Hub will first bring you to one of the many projects which make clear you can't make an iron distinction here between Modernism from below and Modernism from above. Crossing the bridge past Lincoln Hospital, you see a series of enormous slab blocks in a pale, dirty white brick; like many of the housing blocks here, they look like rather cheaper, less imaginative versions of the housing estates of the Brezhnev era. These blocks are what survives of Concourse Village, built as a result of a less metaphorical kind of meat-axe usage. Concourse Village — I suspect the incessant use of the term "village" for parts of a metropolis is at the heart of much of what is wrong with this city — was a co-operative sponsored by and built for the workers of the Amalgamated Meat Cutters union. The massive blocks there now are a truncated stump of "what would have been New York City's largest housing co-operative", according to historian Robert M. Fogelson. It was begun in 1960 as an air rights project over the Mott Haven railyards, not as slum clearance; its building was accordingly, complex, as its builders "had to install more than 1000 concrete columns to support the platform on which the six 25-storey white brick buildings were erected".[10] It was a Mitchell-Lama project, but "sales were slow, in part because many of the prospective purchasers, most of whom were white, changed their minds when they realised they would be living alongside blacks", and "though sales picked up after a while", the scheme was never completed. An ugly billboard at the top gives you the phone number you can call should you wish to buy a flat here.

The transition to the listed, protected section of the Concourse is uneasy, because cars charge down the steep hill on their way to the bridges and tunnels into Manhattan; what could be an elegant townscape, with its elevated, woodsy park and its confidently scaled sweep of apartments (my first thought on arriving at the street was of the affluent West End of Glasgow) is marred by the constant traffic, and the obnoxious kipple which goes with American roadside culture. A drive-thru McDonalds in one direction, and in the other, a billboard with a giant stupid, bespectacled head on it and the words "SUFFERED *PAIN*? YOU NEED *LAW*! 800-PAIN-LAW". The apartment blocks still have some of their glamour, perhaps. But I feel guilty in stating that the part of the Concourse I walked did not altogether send me. It is bookended by some heavy, official buildings of the New Deal era, which emphasise that kinship between 1930s American architecture and that of the interwar dictatorships with less glitz than does Rockefeller Center. The southernmost is the better of them — the Bronx Post Office, built in 1935 like a railway station, a big stone box with massive

Why Not Live in Concourse Village

round-arched windows; it is supplemented by some symbolic WPA sculpture of the postal services; inside are New Deal murals by Ben Shahn, which I was sad not to be able to get in and look at — the building has been part-

Entering a World of Pain

privatised, but rather charmingly now houses a Cuban restaurant on the roof, which was closed as I walked past. Next to it is the more friendly Cardinal Hayes School, a Catholic school in a 1941 Art Deco building with a pair

Bronx Ladies Receive Letters

of handsome if stubby towers either side of a curved frontage — it has a stellar list of alumni, from George Carlin to Don De Lillo to Martin Scorsese. The block at the other end, where I gave up, is the harsh, glowering Bronx

Scorsese High

Grey New Deal

County Courthouse of 1934, a nine-storey, thirteen-bay block, almost a cube, minimal and unforgiving.

Some Light, Some Air

In between are those apartment buildings, and they're fine; evidently New Yorkers, like Parisians, have a tendency to proclaim places that would be considered unworthy of special comment in Birmingham or Lille or Pittsburgh as being great and epic and of world-historical importance. This is a charming trait, but one that can create misunderstandings. The speculative apartment blocks of the Concourse are neither better nor worse architecturally than a UHF co-op, and significantly more interesting to look at than the nasty Concourse Village; their importance, perhaps, is in using the idiom of the Midtown skyscrapers for ordinary housing. Some of these tenements — in the cubic style that in Britain at the time would have been called *moderne*, or *jazz-modern* — look more spruced up than others, and have in some accounts started to welcome young professionals up from Manhattan and Brooklyn. There are great little details, like the Cubist recessed entrances in a series of blocks by the architect-developer Jacob M. Felson; but in general, if this isn't *your* nostalgia then really it's just a very wide street with not enough crossings and far, far too many cars.[11]

The most interesting things that happened on the Grand Concourse as I walked up and down it were strictly non-architectural, as it should be. A group of kids really did pull the lid off a fire hydrant, and leap about in the water, as you would have too if you were ten years old, as it was extraordinarily hot. Actually seeing this quintessential untamed New York street scene was really very touching — we don't do this in south London. I noticed something else on the blocks — several signs for FALLOUT SHELTER with the radiation sign on. At first, I assumed these were some sort of hip, ironic pointers to Cold War-themed bars below, but I saw several of them, and realised that New York still has many of its nuclear shelters, *just in case*. In this, at least, the Sixties never ended.

What If the Cold War Never Ended

A Train Journey
Concrete Capital

"Don't go to DC", I was told by a friend as I expressed my plan to go on a daytrip to the capital during my stay in NYC. "Not in this weather. You won't be able to breathe. It's built in a swamp. Washington is the South." She then paused for a moment — "But then, everywhere south of New York is the South". I can't say I wasn't told. And of course Washington *is* in the South, on various definitions. The District of Columbia stayed on the Union side in the Civil War, but was well south of the Mason-Dixon line. Today, its suburbs stretch into Maryland (in the north in the Civil War), and well into Virginia (in the south in the same conflict; thereby, the Pentagon is in the South). DC has an anomalous political status: notoriously, the capital has no representation in the Senate, a body which blocked a recent attempt to grant it statehood. It was a majority-black city from the 1950s until the 2010s — the *Chocolate City* saluted in Parliament's album of the same name — and there is still an African-American plurality; in the 2020 election, a mere 8% of DC's voters put the X in the box for Donald Trump.

I had one overwhelming reason for going to Washington rather than, let's say, Philadelphia, Boston, Baltimore or New Haven on a daytrip from the metropolis: I wanted to see the Washington DC Metro. As a lifelong public transport user who has never been at the wheel of anything more complex than a dodgem, I am very interested to find notable examples of the form. Friends who had visited the American capital had shown me pictures of immense, atmospheric concrete stations. Given that I was not planning to return to the USA in a hurry, I felt that here was my chance to experience this for myself. But I hadn't realised *quite* what kind of education in public transport I was about to receive. Up early, I took the Subway to the Daniel P. Moynihan Train Hall of Penn Station, the recent conversion to transport use of a postal sorting office opposite the horrible, dark, low-ceilinged, provisional-looking 1960s station (a post-war Modernist building at which I had a look in 2014, and for which I cannot muster even the beginnings of a revisionist case). It is named after the long-standing Democratic senator for New York, famous largely for producing two government reports in the Kennedy-Johnson administrations; one, of 1962, on Federal Architecture, which broke with decades of pompous, retrograde Classicism in favour of something more

Nowhere to sit at Moynihan Train Hall

imaginative; and the other, a 1965 report on black poverty which substantially blamed it on single motherhood.[1]

Architecturally, the Train Hall is a vast improvement on the 1960s station. The restored glass roof, with its huge steel trusses, is a wonderful piece of paleotechnical Classicism, and there's plenty of space. What you will not find are seats, presumably on the off-chance that homeless people might want to sit down, or — shudder — lie down on them. So you wander around for a long time until you decide to join the queue that is stretching, as in an airport, to descend into the underground platform. You then tell a member of staff your seat number, they let you in, write the number down on a bit of paper and stick it in a slot next to your seat; then you wait until 45 minutes later than the advertised time for your train to start moving. The carriage is very spacious, the seats are plush and comfortable, and you have so much leg-room that you could probably use it as a budget sleeper, but beyond that, the appeal of Amtrak's most used line is questionable. In countries where a large proportion of the population regularly takes trains — France, Spain, China, Japan, Germany, *Britain*, even — you do not queue for an hour in a long line — why should you? — you wait in a waiting room, on a seat, like a human being. You then get on the train a few minutes before it departs, which it does, on time.

Unless you take the Acela — the expensive "high-speed" train, which runs at the pace of a normal British intercity train and at around half the speed and all the price of a Shinkansen or TGV — you grind slowly through an ugly landscape of 800-PAIN-LAW-style billboards on motorways, dilapidated clapboard houses and disused factories — a journey enlivened only by the Philadelphia skyline and the welcome relief of Chesapeake Bay. And then, you arrive at a terminus of truly astonishing bombast — Union Station, designed in 1908 by Daniel Burnham, the Chicago architect whose muscular, industrialised Classicism became so popular that it completely supplanted the proto-Modernism of Louis Sullivan in the Midwest city. Burnham's style then spread across the country as an exemplar of the City Beautiful, a distinctly American movement for giant formal Classical ensembles of white stone buildings on green lawns.[2] The first glimpse, as you pass through on your way to the Metro, is jaw-dropping. A delicate, glittering, glass-roofed anteroom framed by chunky Ionic colonnades leads to a coffered double-level arcade, and then gives way to the Great Hall, a space of genuinely dumbfounding scale, gilded and immense. Long before the USA created its post-1945 global Empire, this is grandeur and display in the manner of the most munificent and perverse of Roman potentates. In all this awe you barely notice two odd things. The first is how few people there are — even given that people were only slowly returning to public transport as COVID-19 receded, considerably less people were here than I might expect using the main station in Coventry or Leeds; and second, how oddly joyless the detailing is — this is as mechanised a product as any Modernist building. Then you come out, and you're right on axis with the dome of the Capitol.

The station was the first completed part of a wider City Beautiful project to finally execute the elegant neo-Classical city envisaged in the 1790s by Washington's original planner, the Frenchman Pierre Charles L'Enfant. The 1901 "McMillan Plan" — named after the senator who commissioned it, not the team of planners, which included Burnham, Mead McKim and White, and Central Park's designer Frederick Olmsted — carved a formal capital out of a place which had been regarded by many visitors as little more than a geometric shantytown clustering around the Capitol; the city you can see in front of you, white buildings, green lawns and open space, is theirs more than L'Enfant's.[3]

The Arcade leading to....

...the stupefying Great Hall

City Beautiful plans have been terrible for public transport in many places,[4] and DC's original station was more central, but this is hardly a peripheral location — just there in the near distance is the thing you've come to see as a tourist, and in the plaza in front is the Liberty Bell, whatever the fuck that is. Symbolic figures of gilded-age power represent "Fire, Electricity, Freedom, Knowledge, Agriculture and Mechanics". You have now learned something you will not have noticed in NYC, Grand Central aside — the USA used to create public transport architecture of outrageous splendour. The entrance to Metro will show you something else, too — that it could be created in the 1970s as well, the decade of financial disaster and social democratic degringolade.

I spent the next hour or so just zipping around the Metro, enjoying every moment of the experience — rivalled only by Moscow, Kyiv, Montreal and Stockholm in its aesthetic pleasure. What hits you first is a sense of incredible mass and strength — more convincingly than the Fallout Shelters of the Grand Concourse, these halls feel like they could survive a nuclear war (and, no doubt, this was part of the calculations). The architecture by Harry Weese is unified across the inner-city stations opened in 1977, with only minor variations. Deep escalators deposit you in vast concrete halls, resembling those of Union Station without the gilt and the pomposity, with beautifully finished coffered ceilings in the most brute of *beton brut*. Interchange stations are yet more Piranesian, with chunky Brutalist walkways carrying you across the vaults at Gallery Place, and a change in the ceiling's coffering demonstrating the transition between lines at Metro Center. Trains are fast and frequent retro-futuristic Seventies remnants, and the colourful, schematic and almost instantly understandable abstract map, designed in the Harry Beck-Massimo Vignelli manner by Lance Wyman, hired on the strength of his map

YES

for Mexico City's Metro, is a little "look what you could have won!" aimed at NYC.

It is an astounding achievement, made at a time when it was regularly alleged that the state — the Federal Government in particular — was incapable of executing public projects well, especially projects on this scale. But then Union Station was a precedent for the Metro in more ways than just the coffering — that there was already a station of true if kitsch beauty in the centre of the city, which had escaped the bulldozer, suggested more than the bottom line was at stake in the capital; a place always envisaged as a laboratory, a showpiece. But even then, the DC Metro is remarkable for the degree in which it breaks with American post-war practice. After 1945, the US state spent a ton of money on building freeways and subsidising suburban mortgages, and otherwise let the real estate

Changing at Metro Center

industry develop its enormous, sprawling conurbations. And then, somehow, it did *this*.

According to its historian Zachary M. Schrag, the Metro is the lasting monument of what in the Sixties was called

Changing at Gallery Place

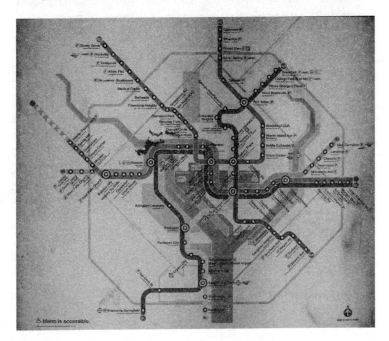

Take That, MTA

the "Great Society", a brief ten-year period in which the American central state made a little attempt to spend some of the immense wealth the country had accumulated on its poorer citizens. In his history of the project, Schrag tries to explain the Metro's alien values to twentieth-century Americans shaped by four decades of neoliberalism:

Metro was never intended to be the cheapest solution to any problem... it is the product of an age that did not always regard cheapness as an essential attribute of good government. To those who celebrate automobile commuting as the rational choice of free Americans, it replies that some Americans have made other choices, based on their understanding that building great cities is more important than minimizing average commuting time.

Moreover, the Metro's approach of unifying a city and making it accessible to all of its inhabitants differs from a communitarian, philanthropic form of urban activism which believes in small-scale solutions to the exclusion of all else and a form of means-testing to make sure that "taxpayers" only subsidise those at the very bottom: that is, "radicals who believe that public funds should primarily — or exclusively — serve the poor, which in the context of transportation means providing bus and rail transit for the carless while leaving the middle class to drive". Moreover, the Metro redresses, albeit quietly, the New York Ideology's hostility to projects as a means of achieving social goals: "to those hostile to public mega-projects as a matter of principle, [the Metro] responds that it may take a mega-project to kill a mega-project".[5]

The Metro was a Kennedy-era project, brought to fruition under Johnson and Nixon, and with some cross-party support — though it was opposed by some local vested interests, such as the head of the city's private bus company, as a "socialistic" system.[6] According with the terms of Moynihan's report on Federal Architecture, it was to be done *well*, not cheaply. The winner of the architectural competition, Harry Weese, proposed stations with spacious vaults, intent on creating "underground equivalents of classic nineteenth-century rail stations, with their cast-iron trainsheds".[7] The team of architects and engineers were sent on a tour of European metro systems, and were inspired by the cavernous architecture of Stockholm, the simplicity of getting from street to platform in Berlin and the graphic design of Milan; each of these would feed in some way to the DC Metro. The general watchword was Stockholm was what *to* do; dark, congested New York what *not* to do. The name, Metro, was intended to avoid the connotations of the NYC Subway, which then was at the lowest ebb of its public reputation. It narrowly avoided having one of those horrible American acronyms used for other metro systems, such as BART in San Francisco-

In the Vaults

Oakland, SEPTA in Philadelphia, PATH in New Jersey or MARTA in Atlanta; the defeat of this idea may have been due to one bureaucrat facetiously proposing the DC Metro be called Federal Area Rapid Transit.

There was a great deal of opposition to the Metro. It went massively over-budget, which had been expected by its backers — a very unlikely low sum was presented to Congress so they wouldn't block it. All the fashionable trends of urban theory at the time went against the Metro. Jane Jacobs, though she lived her entire adult life in two of the North American cities with the most extensive metro systems (New York and Toronto), was suspicious of subways — too big, too centralised, too project-like. Her public transit enthusiasm was for the StarrCar, an on-request mini-tram proposed in the Seventies and implemented only in a small town in West Virginia — something like the Hyperloop of its day. New Left radicals and neoliberals both published studies arguing the Metro would be a boondoggle, and that an expanded bus network would do the job much better. More defensibly, many black residents of a systematically disenfranchised majority-minority city feared the new system would marginalise them in order to cater for white suburbanites and bureaucrats.

According to Schrag, this latter fear has not been borne out: at the time he wrote the book in the 2000s, exactly the same percentage (9%) of both white and black residents of the metropolitan area took the Metro to work; but "in contrast, African Americans were almost four times as likely to ride buses to work as were whites". His perhaps uncomfortable explanation for this is that the Metro — fast, plush, pleasurable to use — is good enough to convince those who could afford *to* drive, *not* to drive. The buses, stuck in traffic, overcrowded, are not. "Moreover", Schrag writes, "the mixing of classes and races helps keep funding secure; politicians cannot cut Orange Line service to the African American neighborhood of Potomac Avenue without also cutting it to wealthy Vienna".[8] So the Metro is also highly unusual in the USA for being an example of real universalism. The public housing laws passed in the government buildings of this city legally mandated that council flats be unattractive, so as not to compete with the free market. The Metro, on the other hand, was built to be nice, and intended for everyone. It took the battle to the free market of the freeways, and has done so with some success — per capita, more people take the subway to work here than in anywhere else in the USA outside of NYC. It is much less than it could or should be, given the climate crisis Washington has played such a huge part in creating, but by American standards, it is a major achievement.

The American anathema on planning fits strangely in DC, one of the most famous wholly planned *tabula rasa* cities on Earth, laid out by utopian revolutionaries with extreme abstraction on a swamp, as part of a planned, militarised project of land expropriation and ethnic cleansing. No North American city is or can be an "organic" growth in the manner of a London or a Tokyo. I realised here that the American anathema on planning and projecting may be analogous to the British suspicion of cities and sentimental love of the countryside. That cult was developed by the first majority-urban country in history, and still one of the most urban peoples on Earth; similarly, Americans speak of *laissez faire* and the evils of planning, and then lay out a grid of freeways on a swamp or a desert and have Washington pay for its construction.

All that said, you can understand why so many people were suspicious of the state building a big public project in DC by getting out at L'Enfant Plaza and having a look at what slum clearance meant in post-war Washington; this is also a useful way of understanding why there was particular dislike of concrete Brutalist architecture on the part of its social movements. Geometric DC is divided officially into quadrants, and this is the Southwestern. By the 1950s its Victorian houses had become slums, with the majority of the terraced houses having no inside toilets, let alone central heating; it is the place documented in Gordon Parks' famous photographs of an updated "how the other half lives", of misery in the shadow this time not of the Woolworth Building, but of the Capitol, and a walk away from the White House. As a district, Southwestern DC was 60% African-American.

The federal government planned the complete demolition of Southwestern DC, leaving nothing left, destroying every single one of its terraced houses. The ownership of the area was sold *en bloc* to a New York developer, William Zeckendorf; when he went bankrupt it was taken over by a consortium mostly owned by the Rockefellers. A mixed-use project of government buildings and public housing was commissioned by Zeckendorf from the Chinese-American Modernist I. M Pei, one of his first major projects. It was as abstract as you might expect in a place like this, with the buildings all hauled up on pilotis above fast roads, with a unified, sober, Brutalist style, and a blanket use of bare concrete. It was one of the first examples of its kind to show the influence of Moynihan's Guiding Principles for Federal Architecture, to showcase Washington to the world not as a sort of Albert Speer Germania that actually got built, but as a thrusting, Modernist city. That's all fair enough. But the fact remains that thousands of people were displaced here to build the following — an office block for the navy; a luxury hotel; the headquarters of the US Postal Service; and, at the time of writing, the National Spy Museum. The latter is at least fitting, as this is a townscape seemingly designed to be a set for *The X-Files*. Some public housing was built as part of the plan, but the office buildings act as a wall screening the city's working

The Parallax View

class from the lawns and monuments of the National Mall, a measure which was no doubt appreciated when DC rioted after the 1968 assassination of Martin Luther King. Cold War notwithstanding, you have to go to Bucharest — or, as Göran Therborn argues in his typology of capitals, *Cities of Power*, Pyongyang — to find anything like it.

The society that would build such a thing does not sound spectacularly great, but suspend your objections for fifteen minutes and you can find a great deal to reluctantly admire, if you like paranoid, extremely mannered, classically proportioned Brutalist architecture. The best work is by Pei himself and the Czech-American architect Vlastimil Koubek, whose offices and hotels, all with a unified style of gridded shafts and overhanging concrete crowns, are imposing, beautifully detailed, and so devoid of any sentimentality, liveliness or humour that they're almost excitingly inhuman, like the blasts of noise in a No Wave record. The James V. Forrestal Building, a massive complex originally for the Navy and now used for the Department of Energy, fittingly in a petrolhead location along the dual carriageway designed by the New Orleans firm Curtis & Davis, is less elegantly nasty, more standard bureaucratic Modernism with its heavy precast rhythms, and was disliked even by Pei himself, who thought it ruined the way his composition had framed the National Mall. The difference is not of great significance. What they all share, these buildings, is a three-dimensionality which makes them very enjoyable to walk upon as a tourist. Like a totalitarian redesign of London's South Bank, you are always above or below the road line, with criss-crossing angular vistas leading to beautifully desolate plazas. I could not defend it on moral grounds; but on aesthetic ones, it is an Antonioni set waiting for Monica

Navy, Energy, Empty

Vitti to pace around in, an Allan J. Pakula place to be assassinated in.

What makes this all rather sad is that the centrepiece, built a little later, is the department of Housing and Urban Development (HUD), designed by the Hungarian Bauhaus exile Marcel Breuer in 1968. The HUD was intended by the Johnson administration, and more importantly, by the department's first chairman, Robert C. Weaver — the USA's first black cabinet member — as a place from which the obviously enormous inequalities created by post-war housing policy could be tackled.[9] The building snaps out of the rectilinear pomposity of L'Enfant Plaza, instead ostentatiously curving away from it, though sharing the use of pilotis to shun the ground and the ubiquitous sculptured precast concrete panels. In another location, maybe it could be a great public building. Not here, though — the rot has gone too deep, and the processes which brought this thing into being on the site of a working-class residential area are too obvious. Within five years, it was all superfluous anyway — in 1973, the Nixon administration passed a moratorium on all new public housing, and the New York fiscal crisis put paid to the public-private alternative of the Mitchell-Lama programme. Instead, HUD has for nearly all its existence been the place from which the destruction of the USA's rudimentary social housing system has been administered.

Here, you're right on the Mall and can explore the centrepiece of American power and, more relevantly, of American tourism; there are a dozen museums and galleries here, most part of the sprawling Smithsonian Institution. If you like Beaux Arts architecture and treeless lawns — I don't — then you can have fun here. What I found more worthy of note were the Victorian remnants from before the White City was built, such as the red sandstone Gothick of the original Smithsonian building, or the gimcrack mini-Kremlin of the Arts and Industries Building, a temporary pavilion

A Model for Housing and Urban Development

How to Fill a Mean Plaza

of 1879 that has somehow survived the centuries, a P. T. Barnum architecture of glass, steel and coloured clapboard. There is also a Modernist museum here, the Hirshhorn, a stylish modern art gallery designed by Gordon Bunshaft of Skidmore, Owings & Merrill and opened in 1974. Here, I saw a blockbuster show by one of those mythic Seventies New Yorkers, and admired the rotunda of Bunshaft's building, another example of how American modern architects had many ways of interestingly framing a formal concrete plaza.

By now, I had almost run out of time — providing that Amtrak was on schedule, and I was not jaded enough yet to assume it wasn't. But I wanted, before I took the train home, to see Watergate. Not because of Nixon's burglary of the Democratic Party offices in the building — which now appears as an event of inconsequence, lodged between the hell Nixon, Johnson and Kennedy inflicted on Vietnam, Laos and Cambodia beforehand, and the subsequent cross-party consensus on austerity and neoliberalism which threw inner-city and industrial America into a misery not seen since the Depression. The burglary's role in Nixon's impeachment was surely on the level of Al Capone being done for tax evasion. No, I wanted to see the building itself. To get there, you take the Metro to Foggy Bottom, admire a few Georgian houses, pass the gross Saudi Embassy and a new street sign reading "Jamal Khashoggi Way", cross a traffic island which houses a tent city of homeless people — a Hooverville, they used to call it, presumably this is a Trumpville or Bidenville — take a bridge over a freeway, ignore the naff classical Modernism of the Kennedy Center for the Performing Arts, and then enter Watergate.

Watergate was designed by the Italian architects Luigi Moretti and Mario di Valmarana for an Italian developer, with the financial backing of the Vatican, on a swampy canal-side site in 1964; it was completed by 1972 and burgled by presidential request soon after. With

Open the Gate

commendable patrician restraint, the authors of the *The AIA Guide to the Architecture of Washington DC* comment that "some of the detailing borders on the eccentric, but it is generally consistent with the baroque quality of the whole complex".[10] What we have here is what would have been called at the time a *Megastructure*. While that term usually suggested vast rectilinear pyramids of building, like Habitat 67 in Montreal, the Nagakin Capsule Tower in Tokyo or the Brunswick Centre in London, this is a building of endlessly looping, fractal curves. At about the top of the DC height limit at thirteen storeys, it contains a large quantity of different functions within a constant twist and turn of concrete balconies and walkways. Within this baffling interlacing you can find several blocks of luxury co-operative apartments, a shopping mall, a medical centre, a hotel and two office buildings.

Detailing is indeed wilful: balconies and walkways are dressed with overhanging concrete slats, creating a slight and amusing Costa del Sol vibe, while ground floor spaces range from meticulously planted gardens and lawns to a layer cake of fountains on a neo-Renaissance checkerboard. The non-orthogonal geometry is an assault on the sensibilities of this city of straight lines, and makes it clear why it was unwise to burgle somewhere so extremely easy to get lost in. But many generations of evil people have lived here, and seem unconcerned by its architectural oddness; the QAnon conspiracists obsess over mundane pizzerias, but here is surely the ideal place for a satanic metropolitan cult, a place which, as you walk up and along the walkways (I found to my great surprise that nobody will stop you), begins to feel like a villain's lair in a 1990s RPG.

I arrived at Union Station on time, which proved to be foolish. The train was an hour late, giving me plenty of time to ponder the selection of souvenirs from *America! Exclusive FBI Merchandise*. Finally on the train, it proceeded to become ever more ridiculously late as it proceeded northwards. The second-to-last train north, it was relatively busy, though if the seats were not laid out as armchairs nobody would have noticed this; as it was, the train crew had to walk up and down carriages telling people to move their bags off the seats, a measure clearly resented, judging by the huffing of the person I sat down next to. It eventually arrived at Penn Station two hours late; apparently, this is normal.[11] Half-asleep, I made my way to the subway at 1am. Services were running regularly, and the platform had more people on it than were in the whole of Union Station. I waited seven minutes for a train, on which people were giggling, chatting and, I exaggerate not, breakdancing. I was in bed in thirty minutes. Lying there, I atoned silently for everything bad I had ever said and thought about the Metropolitan Transit Authority. The Subway — like the NYCHA's estates — is not *nice*. It smells, it's dirty, it's unattractive. Compared to the DC Metro, it's disgusting. No doubt, most suburban Americans would see it as frightening, and many Europeans — even British ones — will see it as an underfunded, filth-caked basket case. But it has one great virtue, apparently rare around here. It actually fucking works.

Architecturegate

Walk 6
Towers Trickle Down

The category of "borough" does not translate well from London to New York. The first London boroughs — long-disappeared entities like the Metropolitan Boroughs of Hampstead, Camberwell, Poplar — were only a little bigger than villages, and the current thirty-two megaboroughs like Southwark or Newham hover around the populations of Hull or Coventry. New York's five boroughs are — aside from the strange anomaly of Staten Island, which actually voted to secede in the 1990s — enormous. Aside from the two complete islands of Staten and Manhattan, their boundaries are apparently arbitrary — there is no Beltway or M25 or *Périphérique* to decisively sever the Bronx from Westchester County, Brooklyn and Queens from the rest of Long Island. Across the Hudson in New Jersey, Hoboken and Jersey City are far closer to the centre of Manhattan than are much of Queens or the Bronx, or any of Staten Island, but state lines being sacrosanct, they have never been brought into NYC's city boundaries. The scale of four of the five boroughs is baffling at first. Queens on its own would be the fifth largest city in the USA; Brooklyn, the most populous borough, has nearly three million inhabitants, which would make it the third largest, just below LA. It would be vast also in Europe — Brooklyn has roughly the population of Madrid and slightly less than Berlin.

Manhattan is appealing to visitors for many reasons, but one of them is surely how quickly you can grasp its structure

— a tall thin island, with a big park in the middle, an upper west, a lower east, the Villages and the Harlems as easily understood points of identification (although few seem to know what happens north of Washington Heights). But in Brooklyn, there is no obvious north or south or centre with which to orient yourself, aside perhaps from the beach in and around Coney Island, which sadly I did not visit. I did little more than dip a toe in the borough. My first was in Downtown Brooklyn and the adjacent district of Brooklyn Heights.

"Brooklyn", like, say, "Hackney", has become a one-word synonym for hipsterism and all that comes with it, and also, for being a place where young people might be socialists, and in a way which is in some whit inauthentic. Naturally, this must obscure as much as it reveals; around half of the London Borough of Hackney consists of council estates of deep poverty, and similarly, it seems from asking around that you will find very few ironic moustaches or homemade modular synths in the Brooklyn districts of East New York or Brownsville. While I am very sure I only scraped Brooklyn's surface, I did see a few things and walk in a few places. I found the "centre" of Brooklyn — as in, the high-rise office area that directly faces Wall Street across the East River — to be an extraordinary mess; in its cacophonous mix of grand civic architecture and gimcrack luxury high-rises, crashing together with no apparent logic, it made me think less of Hackney and more of Britain's deeply weird and uncomfortable new post-industrial high-rise districts, like the Elephant and Castle, Nine Elms or the new centres of Leeds and Manchester.

Stepping out of Borough Hall station — with its delightful polychrome tiles depicting the building it serves — you first see one of the proudest and also most beautifully generic nineteenth-century town halls, a Greek temple of the 1840s with a rather awkward, mildly Baroque spire on top of it. I saw many people were sat on the massive hierarchical flight of steps, a comforting reaction to the authoritarian architecture. There's a great deal more in this vein, Classical monuments on the scale that befits what was for a long time an independent city; two of these are for financial institutions based here rather than in Wall Street, such as the strict, hardline Renaissance palazzo of the 1922 South Brooklyn Savings Bank or the more bumptious dome, portico and Verdigris dressing of the Dime Savings Bank of Brooklyn, built in 1908 and easily imaginable below some skyscrapers over the river. Growing out of the latter today, you will find Brooklyn Tower, the tallest tower in the city outside of Manhattan, the most obvious of a sudden rash of skyscrapers in the borough.

Brooklyn had skyscrapers at the interwar peak of the form, in a cluster facing the river. These sprout up in and around Borough Hall, mostly stolid and unspectacular —

Civic Architecture in Dirty Tiles

with the exception of the fabulously undisciplined Court Chambers Building, a tiered, cranked, spired tower in brown brick which resembles nothing more than one of the towers of the Kremlin after having been sprinkled with some magic fairydust to force it to leap into the skies. It is the major work of the otherwise wholly obscure architect Abraham J. Simberg, who was born in Ukraine in 1892. The Court Chambers Building's completion on the eve of the Wall Street Crash was both the culmination and the end of the architect's career; he was never even paid his full fee for this dreamy, wildly illogical edifice.[1] After the Wall Street Crash, that was it, and no Rockefeller Center would leap in to save Brooklyn's big business. There were no more skyscrapers in the borough (bar a few fairly dull and not particularly tall office blocks and educational buildings) until the Second Gilded Age of the 2010s and 2020s, during which they have emerged at a rate of one every couple of months. Brooklyn Tower is the tallest, by SHoP Architects, designers of some of those pencil towers facing Central Park. This is for a similarly plutocratic clientele. While those towers, those simple rectangular shafts, have a certain monomaniac evil, this tries to rise tier-by-tier like one of the pre-Crash Zoning Code towers of the Twenties, but just looks cruel and nasty, angled and spiked like an instrument of torture. The others, like the rippling 11 Hoyt, by Studio Gang, look less ostentatiously cruel, but the effect is the same — statements that Brooklyn is very much for sale.

In the shadow of these is one of two DSA-aligned young socialist magazines based in Brooklyn, who I was in the borough to visit. It is based in Brooklyn Heights, right in the direct shadow of the new skyscrapers, which loom down on a more domestic scene of low-rise tenements, Greek Orthodox churches and synagogues. This one has a younger editorial team, better graphic design, lower word

The dream of Abraham J. Simberg

counts, neat homemade Constructivist furniture and a sign at the entrance reading "SOCIALISM IN OUR TIME".

The next day, I met up with an editor at the other of these two magazines, in Manhattan; before we went to the

Brooklyn Tower and 11 Hoyt, framed by some Vibrant Street Art

office in Brooklyn he wanted to show me some Brutalist housing in Manhattan as a treat. And it was: he had chosen Waterside Plaza, a superb Mitchell-Lama development right on the East River, near the UN and facing Long Island City. But before the treat, some punishment. The walk there passed through a housing development which was notorious in the middle of the century — Stuyvesant Town-Peter Cooper Village, usually just shortened to "Stuyvesant Town", or in estate-agent-ese, "StuyTown". It hits you soon after you leave your Subway station — a mindboggling 77 (some sources say 110 — nobody seems to have made a precise count) brick slab tower blocks, each of twelve or thirteen storeys, built between 1942 and 1947. It was developed as a "public-private partnership", in which the market, in the form of Metropolitan Life Insurance, was guided by the state, in the form of La Guardia and Moses, to "solve" Manhattan's housing crisis at one massive stroke; rents were kept at a "middle-income" rate, at least until a recent buyout, and the complex has always been popular with residents. But those who hated it practically founded the New York Ideology through their curses upon Stuyvesant Town.

One curse is architectural. Looking at it from the narrow, vertiginous and malevolently anti-pedestrian bridge over Moses' FDR Drive, a freeway severing this part of the city from the river — "like a drawbridge over a moat", as Paul Goldberger puts it — Stuyvesant Town looks horrible.[2] Much more harsh than Queensbridge (and sharing its 25/75% buildings/greenery coverage), it barely even counts as architecture. The towers are as unrelieved by detail, balconies, glass or any notable interest in aesthetics whatsoever, making hard-nosed socialist functionalists like Herman Jessor and the UHF look like prissy aesthetes by comparison; everything possible must have been removed to make it all cost-effective for MetLife. A kinder interpretation might be that all this was an attempt to negate the provisions of the Wagner-Steagall Act that public housing be of a standard low enough for it not to compete with private, by building market housing that had an almost identical design to that of public housing. The only visual quality is one of repetition, the identical slabs marching in a somewhat diverting percussive lockstep. Up close, they are full of green space and gardens, which is why the estate has always been popular. The actual architect of Stuyvesant Town was one Irwin Clavan, but the architect who has always been blamed for it is Le Corbusier. Indeed, in 1942 nowhere had gone as far in trying to implement the Swiss architect's *Ville Radieuse* than this; if the consensus in the 2020s is that Le Corbusier was a great architect and terrible planner, New York spurned the sensuality, wit and drama of his architecture while firmly enforcing his

Radiant City

planning principles, with the identical towers angled to get plenty of light and air, all in a great landscaped park. Metropolitan Life's chair drew attention to this in the publicity: "Live in the Country in the Heart of New York".

The other curse was political. Unlike the informally divided public housing of the time, Stuyvesant Town was *formally* segregated: written into its legal structure was a bar forbidding "Negroes" from moving into the towers; to head off criticism, MetLife built a very similar public-private development in Harlem, Riverton Houses — "separate but equal", a Radiant City of Apartheid. A campaign to desegregate the two developments, beginning with a bill tabled by the Harlem Communist councilman Benjamin J. Davis, saw the provisions eventually removed, but both estates are still mainly white and black eighty years later. Then there was the combined politico-architectural curse, the one that helped found the New York Ideology.

Stuyvesant Town was one of the projects that Jane Jacobs named and described at withering length in *The Death and Life of Great American Cities*. She cites one resident's shock upon watching the estate's security guards move on two twelve-year-old Puerto Rican boys who sat harmlessly talking to each other on one of the park benches of this park city.[3] For Jacobs, this racism had been *created by the buildings' planning* — a suspicion of outsiders that was inherent to Stuyvesant Town's notion of "a city within the city". It was also visually boring, and so low-density as to actively discourage street life and an economy of vibrant small shops: despite its ultra-urban high-rise appearance, the project

> has a density of 125 dwellings per acre, a density that would be on the low side for Greenwich Village. Yet to accommodate so many dwellings as this... the dwellings must be rigidly standardised in rank upon rank of virtually identical, massive elevator apartment houses. More imaginative architects and site planners might have arranged the buildings differently, but no possible difference could be more than superficial. Mathematical impossibility would defy genius itself to introduce genuine substantial variety at these low ground coverages with these densities.[4]

A whole city like this could be terrible; but, as at Co-Operative Village, there is enough of the older city around and nearby that I find it hard to imagine that Stuyvesant Town's residents are particularly impoverished by a lack of bodegas. But the more remarkable point is the cock-eyed spatial determinism — American racism is, apparently, the consequence of Modernist planning.

Waterside Plaza, designed by Davis, Brody and Associates and completed in 1973, is much better, showing that modern architects here were capable of self-correction, and could create something richer texturally, more complex spatially, and by rolling out these innovations on a smaller site, could do so without worrying about the entire venture collapsing financially. In that sense, it confirms some of the wisdom of the Mitchell-Lama plan for affordable housing, in sprinkling it across the city in small high-rise developments rather than through one colossal steamroller. It consists of just four — much taller — towers, which are at the head of an entire swathe of artificial ground, sitting on ballast taken from the Blitzed British city of Bristol, shipped across the Atlantic. The towers, and the low-rise complex of shops, community facilities and maisonettes beneath them, are detailed in redbrick and are subject to a series of Expressionistic bends and twists, carving out of standardised components a dramatic, Gothic skyline. It looks robust, well-made, and the sense of space and vastness created by the river has a real sublimity to it,

Waterside Plaza Skyline

without any need for imagining the countryside. That is, the high-rise garden city bucolic mode of Stuyvesant Town has been dropped, with a simple asphalt promenade meeting the river, dotted with a few trees but no lawns. This is urban housing, and unafraid of it; but in its coherence and integrity it's a project, not something incremental, accidental or speculative. It is a space, a zone, not an ordinary "part of a city".

I was grateful for being shown around the Plaza, despite panicking on the bridge over FDR Drive, but was interested in how it came into being. Waterside Plaza was a state-subsidised scheme (there is a twin development by the same architect in the Bronx, River Park Towers), one of several Mitchell-Lama estates by the developer and occasional politician Richard Ravitch. As it reached maturity, this project was indeed privatised as normal market-rate housing by its residents, which is the snag in the entire endeavour.

Plaza of Waterside Plaza

NYCHA's lack of a Right to Buy has secured a continuous if scarce supply of decent housing for many poor New Yorkers, but the loophole in Mitchell-Lama means that housing for upper-working/lower-middle-class residents has suffered the exact same startling decline as council housing in inner London. Around two thirds of Mitchell-Lama projects have been privatised. Moreover, the scheme's financing methods helped to strengthen rather than weaken the city's extremely powerful property development lobby. New York state did not itself build housing for "middle-income" (i.e., upper-working-, lower-middle-class) people, but through Mitchell-Lama it paid developers loads of money and gave them loads of tax abatements so they would do so; after two or three decades, they could become just another private development. It was predictable that, in a site like this, next to the United Nations headquarters, Waterside Plaza would do so. Ravitch became very wealthy from Mitchell-Lama, although at least he did not have the bad taste to name his affordable housing estates after himself, unlike the German-American Ku Klux Klan supporter Fred Trump, the developer of one of the largest Mitchell-Lama projects, Trump Village in Brooklyn, who bequeathed his property fortune to, well, we know who.

Mitchell-Lama is gone as anything more than a legacy, but the idea that public-private partnerships are the way to solve the failures of the free market in housing endures here. Opposite Waterside Plaza, you can take a good look at Long Island City in Queens, which lacks the coherence for better (Waterside Plaza) or worse (Stuyvesant Town) opposite — a random collection of highly forgettable speculative towers. The very online YIMBY! movement likes to praise this sort of thing as a potential solution to the housing crisis, but as David Madden and Peter Marcuse point out, luxury housing in NYC is still heavily subsidised: "due to the vagaries of local development policies, owners of these buildings frequently pay little or no tax", citing one of the pencil towers south of Central Park, which "received more than $65 million in public subsidies and tax breaks", due to "the idea... that developers of luxury buildings can be incentivized to construct less-exclusive units as well".[5] In Long Island City, 13,000 flats were built: 95% of them are luxury housing.[6] The trickle can be named as a percentage: 5%.

We left Waterside Plaza, crossed that awful bridge, took the Subway, changed, and then arrived at the offices in Greenpoint. He gave me some books, one of which, by the talented essayist Ari M. Brostoff, contained the following explanation of what I had just seen at Stuyvesant Town, stated plainly:

> New York's 20th century high-rises are black boxes, concealing class differences behind a uniformity of ugliness. There are private developments, low-income projects run by the city and middle income co-ops run by the state... complexes built by unions as worker housing and complexes built by socialist organisations for their members.[7]

That is, the social democratic era in New York did not entail everyone living in the same housing, far from it. What it *did* entail was all the housing trying to look the same. The magazine, meanwhile, has a somewhat older editorial team than the other one, more "tasteful" graphic design, more generous wordcounts, no homemade furniture, and a sign at the entrance reading "UTOPIA IN OUR TIME".

Its offices were in Greenpoint, about which the *WPA Guide* informs you: "Greenpoint is the birthplace of Mae West, the actress. The district's residents are credited with originating the widely publicised 'Brooklynese' diction, wherein 'erl' stands for oil and 'poil' for pearl".[8] Today it was, I had been told, a "Polish" area: sitting down in a local cafe to my Chłodnik I was pleased to find this meant actual Polish people live here, as opposed to American Catholics pronouncing their names Sipowicks or Prezbelousky. Outside the Subway station is a delightfully kitsch derelict building housing something called "Polonaise Terrace", depicting a uniformed waiter holding a platter, caked in graffiti. The townscape is good, ordinary, tough urban stuff, redbrick tenements and warehouses, one of them featuring the most bulbous, oversized water tower I had yet seen; but that aside, this is clearly not a place for monuments. A couple of stops away on the Subway was the one thing I most wanted to see in Brooklyn.

Williamsburg Houses is one of two public housing schemes built at the highpoint of the New Deal in New York that were funded by the New Deal's Public Works Administration (PWA).[9] They were greatly trumpeted at the time, including by the *WPA Guide*, which noted the elaborate social life of the

Are You Being Served?

Daddy Water Tower

estate, interestingly given the alleged impossibility of such things in planned developments:

the cultural activities are held in the social and craft rooms of the project and in the community centre of the high school... (NYCHA) provides space for classes for mothers in child care and psychology, men's and women's clubs, a glee club, a tenant's council, and youth groups, but these activities are initiated and conducted by the tenants themselves. The tenants also publish a semi-monthly paper, the *Projector*[10]

That word *"project"*, with its air of the bravely provisional, uncertain and fearless, taken not as an insult but as a badge of honour. Later, Williamsburg Houses was one of two estates to be retrospectively regarded as the road not taken; both commenced before the Wagner-Steagall Act offered more money and attached more strings to socialised housing construction (the other, Harlem River Houses in Manhattan, we will come to presently). Neither was legally segregated, although in practice integration was tokenistic, with just one black family given a flat in Williamsburg Houses at its inception; in reality, one estate was planned as Jewish, the other planned as African-American. Today both are multicultural, majority-minority, black, Hispanic and Asian, with small to non-existent white populations.[11] American racial politics aside, the place is impressive. A walk around Williamsburg Houses will not disappoint: this is as good mass housing as you would get anywhere in the world, at the time or since. If I had to live anywhere in this frustrating city, it would be here.

Walking around it, you'll notice first that Williamsburg Houses doesn't at all resemble the monolithic, institutional look of Queensbridge, Stuyvesant Town and their ilk. The blocks are only four storeys high, without lifts, in yellow brick in a grey concrete frame, with blue tiled corners where the entrances are; the windows are large, and often on the corners of the buildings, to angle more light inside — a

Brooklyn Constructivism

A Road, not Taken

reasonable alternative to the usual lack of balconies. The trees have matured, and offer the same shelter and repose as in Queensbridge, but the way the planning creates several flowing miniature squares is much more attractive, less vague; pedestrian paths also run under the buildings, an intriguing townscape effect created with simple, Modernist means.

The elegant Art Deco signs, the streamlined shops that meet the ordinary tenement streets around, and the zippy Constructivist angularity of the buildings all share in the qualities of the best Manhattan architecture of the time — this is public housing which doesn't look embarrassingly impoverished next to Rockefeller Center. Long before the notion of "trickle down", it shows how the city was for a brief moment able to redistribute at least some of its immense wealth with reasonable fairness, at least in pockets.[12] The architecture of Williamsburg Houses is a *moderne*/International Style collaboration, yoking together the luxury style and its more austere successor — the lead architects were Richmond Shreve, co-designer of the Empire State Building, and the Swiss Modernist William Lescaze, designer of the first International Style skyscraper, the PSFS building in Philadelphia. Their plan broke with the grid system for the first time, its four-storey blocks distributed in green space and angled towards the sun, but that aside, Williamsburg Houses appears to have been anything but influential. In London around the same time, the émigré Soviet architect Berthold Lubetkin told the press that "nothing is too good" for the working class. In the USA, the opposite conclusion was reached — that places like this were just too good, too stylish, too attractive, for working-class people. Build too many Williamsburg Houses, and like the Washington Metro, you could start to convince people that things could be different; that is, you would *compete with the free market*. But then, what also happened next in New York was that the free market, too, created places much worse than Williamsburg Houses. It was the road not taken for everyone.

Walk 7
Three Letters

The young socialists of America can often be found in search of a useable past. This is not unusual for American radicals, who like to evoke the utopian rural communes, the class wars in the mining towns, the strike waves in the cities, all suppressed in an official story of aspiration and individualism and given their due in books like Howard Zinn's phenomenally popular *A People's History of the United States*, published in 1980 when heroic defeats were all that American radicals had left. But, being interested in power — in those forces which *built shit* — the younger generation have tried to understand what they can salvage from the American welfare state, particularly in the moment when it was still in formation during the New Deal. It is no accident that the American new left's policy programme is summed up in the phrase "*Green New Deal*". Of course they're not alone in this — in the UK, the Spirit of '45, the NHS and the age of mass council house-building were all reclaimed as the origin story of the now-scattered and crushed Corbyn movement. But in the USA, it's uniquely difficult, because the creation of the US welfare state was so tied up with the country's rise to becoming an imperial power. If you dig, you can find the colonial undersides of the British welfare state, but no digging is necessary in the United States — it's all on the surface.

In *Fear Itself*, one of the more challenging recent histories of the New Deal, Ira Katznelson presents it as a coalition between urban social democrats and southern rural conservatives utterly committed to segregation and to capitalism, necessary to head off the threats of capitalist collapse and fascist advance, but mostly of note for creating the first really unified federal American state. That state's power was diffused through a series of three-letter public bureaucracies, almost all created by the Roosevelt and Truman administrations. The left can build itself on the rock of the WPA, the PWA, the UHF, even the UDC; but the same people created the CIA and the FBI. However, in the defence of this useable past, the former were dissolved, always seen by most Democrats during the New Deal and the Great Society as mere emergency stopgaps to fix a dysfunctional American capitalism. The WPA could be discarded when the crisis of capitalism was over, and it was. The authoritarian institutions founded at the same time have survived and thrived. How different the country could have been if that was not the case is a nice question, but not a historical one. So on my last day I went to three building complexes which could be seen as representative in some way of the golden age of American social democracy — one in the Bronx, one in Manhattan, the last in Queens. Each of them are unimaginable in America today, but for totally different reasons.

The first was further north in the Bronx from the Opera House Hotel, a Subway ride away, mostly on dramatic elevated steel viaducts. From these, you can get the panoramic view of the borough that punctuated the apocalyptic New York cinema of the late Seventies and early Eighties. The Bronx is no longer a wasteland, but the effect is still much more redolent of a city which has been carpet-bombed than one that has been attacked from the air just the once, twenty-two years ago. It is still a little eerie: in places, the townscape resembles those stretches of Berlin where the Wall once ran, and where tenements and public housing are abruptly broken up by an array of polite and often rather cheap new buildings, and stray open spaces. In amongst these is one of the last projects of Ed Logue: Charlotte Gardens, where he worked with a Bronx community activist group to build a few rows of very simple prefabricated houses of the kind being offered in the outer suburbs — rather pleasant-looking, but an astounding comedown from Roosevelt Island; in the 1980s, if you wanted to build better housing, this was all you could get away with. You also pass the Cross-Bronx Expressway, which did so much damage to the Bronx, sparking off its precipitous decline. You barely notice it. This, as Marshall Berman argued in his immortal passages on the expressway, was the point — cuttings meant that "the Bronx's dreadful fate is experienced, though probably not understood, by hundreds of thousands of motorists every day." What they would have found if they could see it consisted of "hundreds of boarded-up abandoned buildings and charred and burnt-out bulks of buildings; dozens of blocks covered with nothing at all but shattered bricks and waste".[1] That landscape is now gone.

Get off at one of these high-level stations, its viaduct casting welcome shadows on the parched asphalt, and you can find a place which fits neither into Robert Moses' austere, road-focused, Olympian Modernism, nor Berman's Times Square utopianism. The United Workers Co-Operative on Allerton Avenue was built in 1926, to designs by Herman Jessor's firm, Springsteen and Goldhammer. It is one of many co-operatives built by socialists in the northeast Bronx in the mid-1920s, with Abraham Kazan beginning his career in housing at the Amalgamated Houses, and Labor Zionists having their own co-op, Sholem Aleichem Houses. What makes the United Workers Co-Operative unusual is that it was built not by radicals, left-liberals or moderate socialists, but by Marxists: garment workers who were all members of the Communist Party USA. Revolutionaries, committed in word and deed to the destruction of American capitalism — the great enemy towards whom the Red Scare of 1920 and the McCarthy decade were directed.

The Communists, too, built for themselves, and created their own enclave in the city — from the bottom up, democratically, without anyone's permission. Vivian Gornick writes about the "coops", as it was known — without the hyphen — in *The Romance of American Communism*, in 1977: "there are a few thousand people wandering around America today who became Communists because they were raised in the Co-Operative Houses on Allerton Avenue", a place with a rich associative life intrinsically linked to its Communism: its residents "experienced the place as a thriving world whose wholeness of values and activities dominated their sense of being"; its community centres were alive with activity all day and well into the

Why a Duck

night.[2] It had a short life as a co-op, with the co-operators facing bankruptcy in the Depression and forced to sell up to a private landlord, but the residents stayed, and well into the Fifties it was known as a Communist stronghold: "the commie coops".

It is not quite a "black box", in Brostoff's terms, either. The design of the United Workers Co-Operative — like the nearby Amalgamated or Sholem Aleichem Houses — is in a peculiar style which could perhaps be best described as Finno-American Art Nouveau, very distant indeed from Jessor's later austerity. Most of each block is brick, but the rooftops and doorways are in red rubble sandstone, granite and brown half-timbering, in a dreamlike style that evokes most of all the housing architecture of Helsinki or Riga; the *WPA Guide* criticises it for "an ill-advised attempt to put 'cute cottage' feeling into so large a housing group", but after decades of brick boxes, this feels like a non-Modernist analogue to Williamsburg Houses in its unashamed statement of public communal luxury, that *nothing is too good*. The estate's political identity has long passed, but it is in good condition today, with the blocks framing a series of green squares of cherry trees, steps and benches. It does connect with "the street", but then breaks itself up into "a project", with interior spaces oriented towards a collective life for the residents. It originally had clubs, sports facilities, libraries and much else, all of them strongly oriented towards scientific socialism. For the commies of the coops, the revolution and housing were inextricably linked, and improving life in the present could be part of the battle to transform it in the future.

The Bronx is not, you'll find, a uniformly negative case for the future of housing reform — the crisis it once faced has left an imprint of community activism and architectural experiment. It has built new social housing, as we've seen in the Hub, and it has made some good use of

Mock Tudor for Marxists

Cherry Tree Communism

its trickles. You can see another example on the train back from the "coops": Via Verde, the Green Way. This is a large, competition-winning 2012 housing complex combining new "low-income" and "middle-income" flats, co-designed by Dattner Architects and the British high-tech architect Nicholas Grimshaw. It is surprisingly impressive, especially compared with La Central in the South Bronx: in fact it looks luxurious, especially compared with so much of what the city has built for the masses over the decades. It is high-rise, but steps down to provide a series of roof terraces, a common room and shared gardens. It went way over budget, and whether that is connected with the USA's labyrinthine PFI-style contracting systems or anything inherent in the mostly prefabricated construction is hard to ascertain. What is undeniable is how good it looks compared with the sinister shafts of the city's new luxury housing, and how much more it resembles a place where human beings might

Nuevo Trato Verde

want to live together. It is even solar-powered — a little fragment of a Green New Deal, perhaps.

Next to it is the NYCHA's similarly scaled Bronxchester Houses, quite ordinary brick facades with an interesting cranked arrangement, evoking the more epic Brutalist housing estates of Europe, completed in 1978. Recently, these have been given a serious makeover, and now look clean and attractive; this is one of the pilot schemes for the city's plans to divest itself of some of its 400,000 public housing units. This seems to have worked well for residents for the time being,[3] but the rhetoric is curious — NYCHA's new programme has been described, positively, as "Learning from London". This might have been a rather good idea in the 1940s, 1950s and 1960s, when it would have meant building good public housing for everyone. Today, it means emulating London's programmes of "estate regeneration" through demolition, rebuilding and infilling, and building market flats to pay for new public housing — something which seemed a great idea in around 2018, but recently caused the bankruptcy of one borough, Croydon. Any Londoner who knows anything about housing knows that "estate regeneration" has resulted in a net loss of council housing, and enormous profits for developers. In fact, post-1979 New York can actually be proud of itself compared to London — not only is there no Right to Buy, there have been no large-scale demolitions of public housing, unlike, say, Chicago, which has demolished most of its stock. And can it *really* be true that one of the richest cities on the planet can't publicly fund a decent mass housing renovation programme, when Katowice or Aberdeen can?

That's where the useable past comes in, again. The next stop was the twin of Williamsburg Houses, Harlem River Houses, funded by the PWA for the then-new NYCHA around the same time in 1936-38. To reach it, you can walk

John L. Wilson's layout for Harlem River Houses

through a storied townscape of the city's black intelligentsia. In one direction is the UDC's Brutalist Riverbend complex, in another MetLife's Jim Crow Ville Radieuse, its twin of Stuyvesant Town, Riverton Square. In her short memoir of growing up within Harlem's artistic middle class, Michele Wallace remembers walking freely and pleasurably through all these "projects":

> We would go on these long crazy walks in the middle of the night, circling the cluster of buildings made up of Harlem Hospital, the Riverton, the Lenox Terrace, the Riverbend, and a local public housing complex. In 1982 it was as brightly lit as 42nd Street is now, and just as gorgeous and safe-feeling, even though it was two or three in the morning.[4]

Nearby is Dunbar Apartments, a housing co-op and contemporary of the United Workers Co-Operative; it also housed a fair few Communists, but this time, their names are legendary — Paul Robeson and W. E. B. Du Bois were both residents of the co-op. Harlem, just as much as the Lower East Side, was a centre for socialist organising in the interwar years — there is a reason why there was a *Communist Councilman from Harlem*. The CPUSA has not a glowing record on all things, but unlike the Socialist Party — whose leader Eugene V. Debs was passionately anti-segregation, but whose local branches were happy to pander to racism when necessary[5] — it was a consistent force against American racism and imperialism. As a result, many of the major figures of black political life had links with the CPUSA.[6] At its peak in the Thirties and Forties, it was also a politically pragmatic force for redressing specific, resolvable grievances. Benjamin J. Davis wrote in his autobiography of how during his two terms as a Communist councilman, much of his efforts went into housing, particularly in advocating for slum clearance, and against MetLife's twin Jim Crow towers-in-a-park complexes. He asserted that this did not at all put his commitment to revolution in doubt:

> Communists are not opposed to reforms. On the contrary, they work constantly for the slightest improvements that can be won within the framework of capitalism... At the same time, Communists believe that the struggle for reforms should be carried on in such a way as to weaken and expose capitalism and to build up the forces that can bring about the replacement of capitalism by socialism.[7]

Harlem had its Communists and its co-ops, then — but Dunbar Apartments, like the "coops", was taken over by the free market when capitalism had one of its crises in the 1930s. Dunbar Apartments' financial backer was in fact John D. Rockefeller Jr, who foreclosed on the complex during the Depression; nobody was going to redistribute *his* wealth.

Harlem River Houses was not owned or operated by a Rockefeller, nor by a segregationist housing developer: it was owned by the city, by a democratically controlled body, to which you could elect socialists and communists, as people — then — did, and which no Rockefeller could foreclose upon. But first, he had to be paid off — the Rockefellers owned the land, and the city paid a million dollars to take it off them. The estate came into being after a decade of campaigning by tenants' organisations in the district, much of it driven by the Communist Party. The Harlem chapter of the *WPA Guide* — written by then-card-carrying Communist Richard Wright — contrasts the Harlem River Houses with the poverty of the district around:

> In New York City's most overcrowded community, Harlem — where Negroes pay as much as 50 per cent of their incomes for rent, where the rent party is an institution, and where the 'hot bed' serves three shifts of sleepers a day — are the Harlem River Houses, a group of apartment buildings that provide more sunlight, fresh air, and certain other advantages of good housing than the residences of fashionable Park Avenue.

It is "the first large-scale modern housing community for low-income Manhattan residents at rents they can afford"; and it was not solely for the "deserving poor" — instead, "only Negroes from substandard dwellings are accepted as tenants".[8]

Architecturally it is, again, very, very good. It is low-rise, four storeys, on an interesting plan that, like Williamsburg

Houses, combines a sense of enclosure with a Modernist green openness. The architectural team was headed by Archibald Brown, and the actual façade design is duller than Williamsburg Houses' Art Deco-Constructivist fusion, flat, laconic and all in the same brick (thankfully, a nice, bright redbrick, not the dirty dun the NYCHA would later favour); here, you can see hints of the blander style that would follow. But the site-planning, the most interesting aspect of the estate, was by a black architect, John Louis Wilson Jr. His layout shows how it is wholly possible to build a project on a human scale, to break up the grid without being monolithic, to make something that feels public and communal without feeling regimented and institutionalised.

Upon completion, Lewis Mumford shouted from the rooftops about what had been achieved here, in a *New Yorker* review simply called "The New Order": for the first

Harlem's New Order

time in Manhattan, here was a project which recognised that "the first principle of modern neighbourhood planning is to reduce the number of streets, convert more open space into gardens and playgrounds, and route traffic around, and not through, the neighbourhood".[9] Now it had been done, nearly all of residential Manhattan could be torn up and rebuilt accordingly. "Most of the city is obsolete by even minimum standards of health and beauty. Why not cart it away and begin all over?"[10] Well, it wasn't the wave of the future after all. A few decades later, Paul Goldberger asked in his guide to Manhattan architecture: "Why, oh why, doesn't all public housing look like this?"[11] What it did mostly look like can be found in the near distance from Harlem River Houses, in the much more dank, monolithic high-rises of NYCHA's 1968 Polo Grounds Towers. As for the future: like the Bronxchester Houses over the river, Harlem River Houses has recently been offloaded by NYCHA to a non-municipal, non-public social landlord. For the first couple of decades, rents and conditions will stay the same, but after that, they may be turned over to the free market. When that happens, I imagine Harlem River Houses will sell very well; the market seldom builds anything this good.

These golden ages were fragments, never a whole, never a society. The society that did exist — the 1950s and 1960s peak of American imperial power, affluence and appeal to the world as a model to follow — can still store up some surprises. Finns have a curiously important role in American modern architecture; Finnish socialists built New York's first small housing co-ops, and a Finnish émigré architect, Eliel Saarinen — architect of Helsinki's magnificent Central Station — moved to the USA to show them how good, sturdy contemporary architecture could be done. His son Eero was a more flamboyant designer, and at that appalling airport, you can find a statement in three dimensions of what American capitalism once promised: a weightless world in which all the bumph of Europe could be discarded as you passed through Arrivals.

Eero Saarinen's 1959 TWA Terminal — which is, of course, what I'm talking about — is now a hotel, after a long period of disuse. Along with the DC Metro, it is one of very few Modernist buildings I've seen in the two American cities I've visited that have, in the words of Rodney Gordon, given me "that feeling from your balls to your throat". Where you feel weak at the knees, where the power and daring of a space make you gasp out loud. It is a concrete shell or womb of outrageous biomorphic sensuality, bending space and time in a manner appropriate to the deeply unnatural experience of jet travel. There is retro tat everywhere (a Twister room! A café called "Intelligentsia Coffee"!) but I don't care. Maybe it will one day be a terminal again: any plausible future without ecological catastrophe would mean Americans taking trains, not jet aircraft, at least in the easily high-speeded stretches between Chicago and Atlanta or San Diego and Seattle. Flights would be reduced to trips across the Atlantic, over the Gulf of Mexico, and perhaps, until there's a maglev across the desert, to the West Coast. When that happens, this place will be just the right size for people taking a flight every few years somewhere very far away. When that happens, it may even feel like a pleasure, not a chore.

The mismanaged high-security mishmash all around shows that American capitalism can't create anything remotely like this anymore. Like Britain, this appears — on my brief and partial acquaintance — as a poor country whose stats are artificially lifted by the immense wealth of a local plutocracy. Globally, American power and significance are inflated by a giant military, the enduring if increasingly puzzling appeal of its culture industry and a lucrative line in dystopian software design. Wondering idly about a greater America ignores that what the rest of the world needs is

Inside the Whale

a lesser America. The New York developer is no longer President (at the time of writing in 2023) but his pledge to Make America's Airports Great Again, like similar pledges to rebuild the nation's infrastructure and its industry, has led to precisely no positive change whatsoever. Joe Biden might make the same trick work, but I doubt it is possible, at least not with the methods at his disposal. So JFK, past the TWA tourist experience, remains as miserable as ever; the USA is still the only rich country where upon arriving in Britain you are met with far better infrastructure than in the country you've departed from. Gatwick will never look so pleasant as it does after JFK.

How this place gets you is by making you believe not in what you see, but in its pure potential, in what it could be. Against my better judgement, then, I will be waiting with optimism for the projects of the future, for the commie coops to come.

Notes

1   Cannibal Ox, "Iron Galaxy", The Cold Vein (Def Jux, 2000)
2   Mason B. Williams, *City of Ambition: FDR, La Guardia and the Making of Modern New York* (Norton, 2013), ebook, loc 378
3   Sting, "An Englishman in New York" (1987)

Introduction: The New York Ideology

1   For an appropriately short-tempered takedown of this framework and its uselessness to New York in the 2020s, see Samuel Stein, "Robert Moses! Jane Jacobs! Robert Moses! Jane Jacobs!" *n+1*, July 21st 2023, online at https://www.nplusonemag.com/online-only/online-only/robert-moses-jane-jacobs-robert-moses-jane-jacobs/
2   No, I haven't read *The Power Broker*. Come back to me when the Pulitzer Prize is awarded to a thousand-page study of Patrick Abercrombie or Konrad Smigielski.
3   Jane Jacobs, "Downtown Is for People", in *The Exploding Metropolis: The Editors of Fortune*, (Doubleday, 1958), p. 142. For a good anthology, see Samuel Zipp and Nathan Storring (eds), *Vital Little Plans: The Short Works of Jane Jacobs* (Short Books, 2017)
4   Respectively, Patti Smith, "Piss Factory" (1975); Grandmaster Flash and the Furious Five, "The Message" (1982).
5   Notorious BIG, "Juicy" (1994)
6   I owe this point to Douglas Murphy.

Walk 1: Paleotechnical Manhattan

1   "Donald Trump is right: America's airports are awful", *The Economist*, September 29th 2016

2   For a fascinating take on the early Ansonia as a sort of luxury communal apartment for rich people, see Helen Hester and Nick Srnicek, *After Work: A History of the Home and the Fight for Free Time* (Verso, 2023)

3   "Downtown is for People", *The Exploding Metropolis*, p. 158

4   Robert Fitch, *The Assassination of New York* (Forbidden Bookshelf, 2014), p. 229

5   Marshall Berman, *On the Town: One Hundred Years of Spectacle in Times Square* (Verso, 2009), p. 203

6   I met Berman once, having invited him to speak at an event at Birkbeck College, London, in 2009. He was very courteous, very hairy and very spaced-out. During one of the other talks on the day he fell asleep, and then fell out of his chair.

7   Samuel R. Delany, *Times Square Red, Times Square Blue* (NYU, 1999), p. 15

8   Ibid., pp. 148-149

9   Elliott Willensky and Norval White, *The AIA Guide to the Architecture of New York City* (Harcourt & Brace, 1988), p. 230. For a recent appraisal of this talented and sinister architect, see Charles Rice, *Interior Urbanism: Architecture, John Portman and Downtown America* (Bloomsbury, 2016)

10 That sense of gloriously aloof disjunction can still be found in other Mies buildings, however, as for instance in Westmount Square in Montreal, which I enthuse about in *Artificial Islands: Adventures in the Dominions* (Repeater, 2022)

11 On these encounters, see Jean-Louis Cohen, *Scenes of the World to Come: European Architecture and the American Challenge, 1893-1960* (CCA, 1995)

12 Samuel Chamberlain, *Rockefeller Center: A Photographic Narrative* (Hastings House, 1940), p. 2

13 Ibid., p.3

14 Christine Roussel, *Guide to the Art of Rockefeller Center* (Norton, 2006), p. 6

15 Ibid., p. 55

16 Ibid., p. 76

17 Susan Sontag, "Fascinating Fascism", in *Under the Sign of Saturn* (Vintage, 1981), p. 94

18 Louis H. Sullivan, *The Autobiography of an Idea* (Dover, 1956), pp. 202-203

19 There is another possible explanation for the building's long obscurity in its industrial/warehousing location — the writers of the authoritative guide to NYC architecture quote the developer as asking, "Who would expect an aesthetic experience on Bleecker Street?" Willensky and White, *The AIA Guide to the Architecture of New York City*, p. 151

20 I cite in my defence Michael Sorkin's appreciation of the building in *What Goes Up: The Rights and Wrongs to the City* (Verso, 2018)

Walk 2: Maps and Conduits

1 See Peter B. Lloyd with Mark Ovenden, *Vignelli Transit Maps* (RIT Press, 2012)

2 Westyard has since, sadly, been reclad in bland blue glass and the tracks covered, as part of the Hudson Yards complex, a new skyscraper development in the Battery Park City vein.

3 Manfredo Tafuri, *The Sphere and the Labyrinth* (MIT Press, 1980), p. 172

4 James Baldwin, "Fifth Avenue, Uptown", in *Nobody Knows My Name: More Notes of a Native Son* (Penguin, 1991), p. 61

Walk 3: The Welfare Island

1 On the young socialists, see Raina Lipsitz, *The Rise of a New Left: How Young Radicals Are Shaping the Future of American Politics* (Verso, 2022). The most convincing account I've read

of this formation — and its complicated class composition, which should be familiar to us recovering Corbynites over the pond — is Chris Maisano, "The Liminal Left's Bid for Power", *Jacobin*, February 2022. On its successes and limitations, the same magazine's special issue "The Left in Purgatory", published the same year, is very instructive.

2 There is a great account of the sheer strangeness of these towers in Justin Beal's memoir-cum-architectural history *Sandfuture* (MIT Press, 2021)

3 Lewis Mumford, "The Modern Hospital", in *Sidewalk Critic: Lewis Mumford's Writings on New York* (Princeton, 1998), p. 63

4 Sert was also the nephew of Josep Maria Sert, one of the kitsch Art Deco painters who decorated the Rockefeller Center; indeed, Sert Sr was the hack painter hired by Nelson Rockefeller to replace — to literally paint over — Diego Rivera's censored murals in the complex.

5 Lizabeth Cohen, *Saving America's Cities: Ed Logue and the Struggle to Renew Urban America in the Suburban Age* (Picador, 2019), p. 257

6 There is a good short account of UDC — and of Rockefeller's betrayal of New York and mayor Abraham Beame — in Kim Phillips-Fein, *Fear City: New York's Fiscal Crisis and the Rise of Austerity Politics* (Picador, 2018)

7 Cohen, *Saving America's Cities*, p. 284

8 Ibid., p. 288

9 Ibid., p. 287

10 Matthias Altwicker, "Eastwood", in Nicholas Dagen Bloom and Matthew Gordon Lasner (eds), *Affordable Housing in New York* (Princeton, 2016), p. 239

11 Bloom and Lasner, *Affordable Housing in New York*, p. 1

12 *The WPA Guide to New York City* (The New Press, 1982), p. 588

13 Figures from Corey Kilgannon, "Amazon's New Neighbor:

The Nation's Largest Housing Project", *New York Times*, November 12, 2018

14 Stephen Petrus and Molly Rosner, *Voices of Queensbridge: Stories from the Nation's Largest Public Housing Development* (La Guardia and Wagner Archives, 2019), p. 17

15 I can't recommend it enough: https://www.youtube.com/watch?v=0eckRNcHCKA

16 Ali Shaheed Muhammad and Frannie Kelley, "Marley Marl on the Bridge Wars, LL Cool J and Discovering Sampling", *NPR*, September 12 2013, online at https://www.npr.org/sections/microphonecheck/2013/09/11/221440934/marley-marl-on-the-bridge-wars-ll-cool-j-and-discovering-sampling

17 Petrus and Rosner, *Voices of Queensbridge*, p. 24; on the support in working-class minority communities for the policies which would cause the mass incarceration of young working-class minority Americans, see James Forman Jr, *Locking up Our Own: Crime and Punishment in Black America* (Farrar, Strauss & Giroux, 2017)

18 On De Blasio, see the calmly devastating chapter on his tenure in Samuel Stein, *Capital City: Gentrification and the Real Estate State* (Verso, 2019). On the sharp, cynical Adams, see *Jacobins* passim, e.g., Ross Barkan, "Eric Adams is the most pro-landlord Mayor New York has had in years", 27th April 2022, at https://jacobin.com/2022/04/eric-adams-new-york-city-pro-landlord-tenants-rent-burdens

19 Petrus and Rosner, *Voices of Queensbridge*, p. 162

Walk 4: Now We Return to Wipe out the Slum

1 Though it was Knickerbocker Village, not Amalgamated Dwellings, that counted Ethel and Julius Rosenberg as tenants.

2 *The WPA Guide to New York City*, p. 116

3 This tradition endures today not only in DSA, but also in the disgustingly-named Working Families Party, founded in

the 1990s to push local Democrats in a more "progressive" direction.

4   The great book on this difference is Gøsta Esping-Andersen, *The Three Worlds of Welfare Capitalism* (Polity, 2013)

5   Michael Harrington, *The Other America: Poverty in the United States* (Penguin, 1963), p. 31

6   Joshua B. Freeman, *Working-Class New York: Life and Labor Since World War II* (The New Press, 2000), p. 103

7   Ibid., p. 65

8   Annemarie Sammartino, *Freedomland: Co-Op City and the Story of New York* (Cornell, 2022), p. 117

9   Robert Fogelson, *Working Class Utopias: A History of Co-Operative Housing in New York City* (Princeton, 2022), p. 31

10 Ibid., p. 83

11 Freeman, *Working-Class New York*, p. 116

12 Cited in James Nevius, "Living in Co-Op City in the Bronx", *Curbed*, December 5th 2018 https://ny.curbed.com/2018/12/5/18126231/co-op-city-rental-apartment-prices-history-nyc

13 Freeman, *Working-Class New York*, p. 118

14 This is also the finding of Annemarie Sammartino's superb history Freedomland, though she does point out that the UHF's Co-Op City was a dull place to be a teenager.

15 Cited in Tony Schuman, "Labour and Housing in New York City: Architect Herman Jessor and the Cooperative Housing Movement", (2010), online at http://urbanomnibus.net/wp-content/uploads/sites/2/2010/03/LABOR-AND-HOUSING-IN-NEW-YORK-CITY.pdf

16 See Cole Cahill, *The Limits of Cooperation: Confronting Privatisation at Limited Equity Co-Operatives in New York City*, thesis, Columbia University, 2023, pp. 18-19.

17 Freeman, *Working-Class New York*, p. 116

18 See Peter Eisenstadt, "Rochdale Village", in *Affordable Housing in New York*; on Co-Op City, see Sammartino, *Freedomland*.

19 Nicholas Dagen Bloom, "Jacob Riis Houses", in *Affordable Housing in New York*, p. 131

20 For an insightful account of how this happened and how it exploited the planning laws of this previously wholly "affordable" area, see Karrie Jacobs, "A tale of Two Bridges", *Curbed*, September 25th 2019, online at https://ny.curbed.com/2019/9/25/20878228/lower-east-side-two-bridges-nyc-zoning-development

21 I asked New York housing authority David Madden why this was the case; his explanation was simple. "Red diaper babies".

22 Cahill, *The Limits of Cooperation*, p. 56

23 Alongside of course the rediscovery of J. Sakai's much more sectarian and bleak, if brilliantly vituperative 1983 history *Settlers: The Mythology of the White Proletariat* (PM Press, 2014)

24 Max Elbaum, *Revolution in the Air: Sixties Radicals Turn to Lenin, Mao and Che* (Verso, 2018), p. 200

25 Jennifer Hock, "Asian-Americans For Equality", in *Affordable Housing in New York*, p. 280

Walk 5: Leftovers from the Meat-Axe

1   I owe this important information to Lillian Knorr, "Hip Hop and Subsidised Housing", in *Affordable Housing in New York*.

2   Statistics from C.J. Hughes, "In the Bronx, Mott Haven Suddenly Gets a Skyline", *New York Times*, October 15, 2021

3   As in the UK, the public-private financing mechanisms that got this built are of mindboggling and stupid complexity: the building's budget came from 17 different sources. Justin Davidson, "La Central may be the best affordable housing your taxes can buy. And that's the problem", *Curbed*, June 30 2021, online at https://www.curbed.com/2021/06/south-bronx-housing-la-central.html

4   Elbaum, *Revolution in the Air*, p. 75

5   Another noteworthy employer in the Hub is Uber, who have

a "Driver Center" in a big box shed near the Hub. On the industry-to-healthcare transition, see Gabriel Winant's *The Next Shift* (Harvard, 2021), one of the best books by the new generation of American socialist writers.

6   Marshall Berman, *All That Is Solid Melts Into Air: The Experience of Modernity* (Verso, 1982), p295

7   Cited in the invaluable, Caro-obviating "Robert Moses" file of Kenneth Goldsmith's *Capital: New York, Capital of the Twentieth Century* (Verso, 2016), ebook, loc 17028

8   Ibid., loc 25575

9   Freeman, *Working-Class New York*, p. 277. This history, incidentally, is why the "urban farms" popular among online environmentalists placed in the devastated interstices of urban America, are not necessarily popular in the local area. As Mike Banks of Detroit's Underground Resistance, one of the great black Modernists, once quipped: "We call them Urban Plantations".

10   Fogelson, *Working Class Utopias*, p. 66

11   But those who want to look further can find detailed descriptions of the buildings on the Historic District designation, online at http://s-media.nyc.gov/agencies/lpc/lp/2403.pdf

A Train Journey: Concrete Capital

1   For a very interesting recent account of this Moynihan Report and its influence, see Touré Reed, *Toward Freedom: The Case Against Race Reductionism* (Verso, 2020)

2   Londoners owe to Burnham the splendid megalomaniac kitsch of the original Selfridges building on Oxford Street.

3   See here *The WPA Guide to Washington DC* (Pantheon, 1983), pp. 60-67

4   Ottawa is a spectacular example, described with horror in my *Artificial Islands*.

5   Zachary M. Schrag, *The Great Society Subway: A History of the Washington Metro* (Johns Hopkins, 2006), p. 21

6   Ibid., p. 102
7   Ibid., p. 123
8   Ibid., p. 363
9   For an interesting recent defence of Weaver and his ideas
     on housing against "race reductionism", see Preston H.
     Smith II, "Race and the Housing Question", *Catalyst*, Spring
     2023.
10   Christopher Weeks, *The AIA Guide to the Architecture of
     Washington DC* (Johns Hopkins, 1994), p. 146
11   For a sharp account by a young North American socialist
     of the problems of public transport in the USA, almost all
     of which have long been solved by most countries between
     Portugal and Japan — and a depressing description of the
     snake oil remedies offered for them by the Californian tech
     industry — see Paris Marx, *The Road to Nowhere* (Verso,
     2022)

Walk 6: Towers Trickle Down

1   An excavation can be found in David W. Dunlap, "A Moment
     in the Limelight, 30 Years Late", *New York Times*, February
     21st 2012, online at https://archive.nytimes.com/cityroom.
     blogs.nytimes.com/2012/02/21/a-moment-in-the-
     limelight-30-years-late/
2   Paul Goldberger, *New York, The City Observed: A Guide to the
     Architecture of Manhattan* (Penguin, 1979), p. 103
3   Jane Jacobs, *The Death and Life of Great American Cities*
     (Pelican, 1974), p. 59
4   Ibid., p. 228
5   David Madden and Peter Marcuse, *In Defense of Housing: The
     Politics of Crisis* (Verso, 2016), ebook, loc 415-424
6   But the money has to go somewhere. "One example was the
     Hayden Apartments by Rockrose Developers. With rental
     units beginning at $2,655 for a studio, residents had access
     to a dog-grooming station, yoga studio, private rooftop

park, library, and a basketball court." Petrus and Rosner, *Voices of Queensbridge*, p. 52

7   Ari M. Brostoff, "The Family Romance of American Communism", in *Missing Time: Essays* (N+1, 2022), pp. 103-4

8   *The WPA Guide to New York City*, p. 459

9   On the PWA housing — and on how the 1937 Wagner-Steagall bill, the project of Modernist social democrats like the critic Catherine Bauer, was sabotaged by conservative Democrats, crushing what was probably the USA's best chance for developing a decent public housing programme — see Gail Radford, *Modern Housing for America: Policy Struggles in the New Deal Era* (University of Chicago, 1997)

10   *The WPA Guide to New York City*, pp. 458-9

11   See Samuel Zipp and Nicholas Dagen Bloom, "Williamsburg Houses", in *Affordable Housing in New York*, p. 98

12   There was also an excellent Constructivist mural in the complex, recently cleaned, removed and put in the Brooklyn Museum — too good for the working class, again. See https://www.brooklynmuseum.org/exhibitions/williamsburg_murals

Walk 7: Three Letters

1   Berman, *All That Is Solid Melts Into Air*, p. 291

2   Vivian Gornick, *The Romance of American Communism* (Verso, 2020), p. 53

3   Nicholas Dagen Bloom and Karen Kubey, "At NYCHA, a Small Project High-Concept Reset", *Gotham Gazette*, September 28 2017, https://www.gothamgazette.com/130-opinion/7223-at-nycha-a-small-project-high-concept-reset

4   Michele Wallace, "Memories of a 60s Girlhood: The Harlem I Love", in *Invisibility Blues: From Pop to Theory* (Verso, 2016), ebook, loc 177-178.

5   Victor L. Berger, the Socialist Party of America leader who built its formidable base in Milwaukee, was notably

regressive on race. On Milwaukee's long-running socialist governments from the 1910s to the 1960s, by far the most extensive municipal socialist experiment in the US, see the glowing chapter in John Nichols, *The S-Word: A Short History of an American Tradition... Socialism* (Verso, 2015), or Gregory Afinogenov's much more unsentimental essay on the subject in Keith Gessen and Stephen Squibb (eds), *City by City: Dispatches from the American Metropolis* (N+1, 2015)

6   This too has started to feature in some revisionist histories — a good one, on the Communism of Robeson, Du Bois, Claude Mackay and Langston Hughes, is Kate A. Baldwin, *Beyond the Colour Line and the Iron Curtain: Reading Encounters Between Black and Red, 1922-1963* (Duke, 2002)

7   Benjamin J. Davis, *Communist Councilman from Harlem: Autobiographical Notes Written in a Federal Penitentiary* (International Publishers, 1969), p. 100

8   *The WPA Guide to New York City*, pp. 392-4. It was not Wright's only work with a New Deal institution: around the same time, Wright was working on *Twelve Million Black Voices* (Lindsay Drummond, 1947), a poetic history of black America with photographs taken from the voluminous documentation of poverty by the Farm Security Administration.

9   Mumford, *Sidewalk Critic*, p. 210

10   Ibid., p. 212

11   Goldberger, *New York, The City Observed*, p. 299

Acknowledgements

All photographs are my own, except those in Walk 2 with (SM) in parentheses, which are by Samuel Medina. This short book was made possible by two invitations to New York, in 2014 and 2022. Thank you to James D. Graham at Columbia University's Graduate School of Planning and Preservation for the former, and to Jeff Rosenheim at the Metropolitan Museum of Art for the latter. Thanks to Lucy Sante for very kindly and flatteringly lobbying on my behalf; to Mark Krotov for walking me around Waterside Plaza and Greenpoint, and for, I hope, forgiving my not submitting this text to him despite it being his idea. Thank you to expatriates Sukhdev Sandhu and Dan Fox for fielding my desperate questions as to why the Subway map is not like a good map, by Harry Beck.

Marianela D'Aprile and Samuel Medina at the excellent *New York Review of Architecture* met me in 2022, and despite it being clear there and then what a noob I was, agreed to read over the manuscript I wrote afterwards. Naturally it is all my fault and not theirs, but I am grateful to both for their very useful suggestions, and in Sammy's case for accepting the assignment to take the photographs for Walk 2. Thank you at Repeater to Tariq Goddard for his eagerness in accepting the idea for this book, to Josh Turner for agreeing to do it quickly, and to Johnny Bull for once again turning one of my questionable cover ideas into a reality. Much of Walk 2 was originally published in *Jacobin*: thanks to Bhaskar

Sunkara for these commissions, and to Polina Godz, Remeike Forbes and everyone else on the democratic socialist rooftop barbecue for fielding rubeish questions. Love to the inestimable Carla Whalen.

REPEATER BOOKS

is dedicated to the creation of a new reality. The landscape of twenty-first-century arts and letters is faded and inert, riven by fashionable cynicism, egotistical self-reference and a nostalgia for the recent past. Repeater intends to add its voice to those movements that wish to enter history and assert control over its currents, gathering together scattered and isolated voices with those who have already called for an escape from Capitalist Realism. Our desire is to publish in every sphere and genre, combining vigorous dissent and a pragmatic willingness to succeed where messianic abstraction and quiescent co-option have stalled: abstention is not an option: we are alive and we don't agree.